How to Choose a
Small Business
Computer System

How to Choose a Small Business Computer System

by

D. Weale

BERNARD BABANI (publishing) LTD
THE GRAMPIANS
SHEPHERDS BUSH ROAD
LONDON W6 7NF
ENGLAND

Please Note

Although every care has been taken with the production of this book to ensure that any projects, designs, modifications and/or programs, etc., contained herewith, operate in a correct and safe manner and also that any components specified are normally available in Great Britain, the Publishers and Author do not accept any responsibility in any way for the failure, including fault in design, of any project, design, modification or program to work correctly or to cause damage to any other equipment that it may be connected to or used in conjunction with, or in respect of any other damage or injury that may be so caused, nor do the Publishers accept responsibility in any way for the failure to obtain specified components.

Notice is hereby also given that if any equipment that is still under warranty is modified in any way or used or connected with home-built equipment then that warranty may be void.

© 1992 BERNARD BABANI (publishing) LTD

First Published — June 1992

British Library Cataloguing in Publication Data:
Weale, David
    How to Choose a Small Business Computer System
    I. Title
    658.05

ISBN 0 85934 323 5

Printed and Bound in Great Britain by Cox & Wyman Ltd, Reading

About the Author

David Weale is a fellow of the Institute of Chartered Accountants and has worked in university administration and chartered accountancy practices (dealing mainly with small businesses). At present he is a full-time lecturer in further education at Yeovil Tertiary College where he lectures in business computing. He also runs and has been known to enter triathlons as a relaxation from computing.

He is married with three children and a Siamese cat and lives in Somerset.

Trademark Acknowledgements

Dedication

To all my family and especially to my father, without whose guidance earlier in my life, this book would not have been written.

Contents

Introduction

This book is intended to assist you in buying and using an IBM compatible computer system. It will be useful whether this is your first system or if you are replacing an old friend (or possibly enemy).

The content concentrates on IBM compatible computer systems simply because they are the standard business machine, although much of the contents are relevant to any system.

It covers all the necessary areas for you to be able to make an informed choice and contains many useful warnings and ideas.

Obviously in a book of this size there is a limit to the level of detail that can be included and there is an appendix detailing other sources of help.

The emphasis is on business use, however this includes anyone getting a system for any purpose other than pure recreation.

There is much fun and satisfaction to be had from computing (even accounting systems) and I hope you enjoy it as much as I do.

With best wishes for your success and enjoyment.

David Weale

Buying A System

How to begin the process

Before going into any detail about the hardware and software you need, you should ask several questions about why a computer system may be necessary to you.

It is unfortunately still true that far too many businesses, both large and small, make expensive mistakes simply because they have not thought carefully enough about exactly what they are trying to achieve.

The questions you need to ask are:

*   Why do you need a computer system and what are you going to use it for.

*   Is a computer system actually going to help your business become more efficient.

You should be as precise as possible, vague ideas about the wonders of modern technology may not actually translate into a cost effective solution.

Try to calculate how much time will be saved using computer technology and what other advantages you expect (for example being able to obtain information that would be unavailable without using a computer).

Work out how much money you can afford to spend on the total package (and stick to it).

Remember that the total may have to include items such as furniture, after-sales support and training as well as the hardware and software, and also new stationery.

Consider whether any government grants are available for any of these costs.

> **Write your answers down on paper**

The answers to these questions will be useful when you discuss your requirements with a computer dealer or consultant.

By reading this book you will gain an understanding of how computers can help your business. However there is nothing like physically using computers and you should read computer magazines, and visit exhibitions and dealers to help you learn and to make the right decision.

If you have time, most local colleges run introductory courses in the evening for the beginner and may also run advanced courses, both daytime and evening.

> As you learn you may find your answers to the previous questions change, so do not be in too much of a rush.

The next stage is to decide how to obtain the system.

There are two options open to you:

*   Use your own knowledge.

        and/or

*   Rely on either a computer dealer or a consultant to make the choices for you (having told them what you want the system to do and how much you can afford).

Where to buy the system

If you look at the computer magazines (the ones which deal with business, not those with colour pictures of aliens on the front), you will be amazed at the variety of firms offering to sell you hardware and software at very attractive prices.

Unfortunately some of these firms are not so helpful after the sale and are essentially box shifters (they sell the system without providing much after-sales service and expect you to have a fair degree of knowledge of PC's).

Since you are buying this system for your business and any problems could affect the running and possibly the profitability of your firm, it is in your best interests to be careful and conservative in your choice of supplier.

There are various guide-lines I would suggest:

Choose either a reputable local supplier (ask around, they are likely to be a member of the local chamber of commerce) or a well known national company which is going to be around for a few years (some of the better known are for example Viglen, Elonex, Dell, Austin and Dan Technology).

Try to find a dealer / consultant who understands your specific type of business.

You can ask for a list of previous clients and contact them for their views of the standard of service and support.

If possible buy locally as it is easier to complain to and get help from a person than a disembodied voice at the end of a phone.

Most local suppliers are enthusiasts who have made a business from their obsession and will go out of their way to be helpful (but remember you cannot expect to get both service and the cheapest prices).

One of the most important areas to check out is the availability of after-sales service, support and training (if necessary). As with most business contracts, get details of this in writing if possible.

You may want to avoid the high street chains who tend to be weaker in the area of technical support either before or after the sale (especially the smaller branches), unless you are in the market for a games machine in which case they may be the best place to buy.

Get all the details in writing before committing yourself. Most contracts specifically exclude verbal statements about the system, so please put everything in writing .

Try to visit as many potential suppliers as possible and discuss your needs with them, it is best to make an appointment first though as the kind of service you will get on a busy Friday afternoon may not be typical of the firm.

Whether to use dealers or consultants

In an ideal world the difference between a dealer and a consultant is that a consultant is totally independent and will give you unbiased advice (for which they will charge you), a dealer may sell only a limited range of goods and will usually want to sell you one of these.

In reality some consultants are tied in with certain suppliers and make their money both from charging you for their time and in commission from the supplier. Be warned. In fact most dealers offer a form of consultancy usually free or at a low cost.

Points to think about

Buy the most appropriate hardware and software you can afford for your purposes. There is little point in buying a state of the art system if all you need to do is word processing and simple accounting tasks. Your needs may develop though so do consider the future.

Get demonstrations of the proposed hardware and software working together, preferably on real life activities rather than demonstration programs (which are produced to give the most favourable impression of the system).

Look at the features of several combinations of hardware and software and compare them. When you have identified a likely system see if you can borrow (or hire) it for a day or so, so that you can test it.

You are only likely to be able to do this if it is a local dealer who is fairly sure that a sale will eventually result. However several national firms offer a 14 or 30 day money back guarantee if you are not happy with the system (although this may only apply to the hardware).

Try to use the system yourself (get your staff to try it out as well and listen to their comments). Items such as the keyboard and VDU can differ considerably from system to system and may have an effect on how happy you are to use it and on your efficiency.

Be guided by the experts (assuming you have found a reliable one). It is not in a local dealer's interests to sell you something unsuitable, especially if they intend to stay in business.

Always take out an annual on-site maintenance contract (and check just how fast the engineer will arrive). You normally cannot afford to pack up the computer, mail it back and wait for it to be fixed. A maintenance contract is an insurance that your system will only be non-operational for a very short period of time. Check if a loan system is available if yours needs major surgery.

Software specifically

When looking at software it is obviously necessary to discover if it will do what you want, however there are other factors which you should take into account:

*   Does it have any drawbacks (from your point of view), for example are there tasks it is unable to do (easily or at all).

*   Does it fit in with your methods of working or will you have to change these to accommodate the program.

*   Is it user friendly (i.e. easy for a novice to use).

*   Are there adequate explanations on how to use the program, look at both the manual and the on screen help.

Possible additional costs

As well as the hardware and software, there are other costs which should be budgeted for:

*   Installation costs, e.g. carpeting, wiring, furniture, etc.

*   Training your staff in the use of the new system.

*   Insurance and maintenance contracts

*   Computer media (discs, headed paper, preprinted invoices, printer supplies).

These can add up to quite a sum over a year.

Training is vital if the most effective use is to be made of the system. This can be carried out by sending the staff on training courses (either commercial courses or those at the local college).

Financing the system

There are alternatives to outright purchase, any of which may be suitable for your particular needs.

Buying

Either directly from your bank account or by a loan. This means the equipment belongs to you, but you will have reduced the working capital of the business and have less money for other purposes.

Leasing

There are various types of leasing agreement and the amount to be paid will vary with the length of the lease. Several firms have started to lease PC's to businesses and it may be a very cost effective way to obtain a system.

Be wary of any penalties built into the contract (for changing the system, etc.) and remember you do not own the system and still have to pay to maintain it.

The major advantage is the low initial outlay, although it may be more expensive in the long run. It does have an additional advantage (if the lease allows it) of being able to change the equipment whenever necessary (thus avoiding technological obsolescence).

Renting

This can be expensive in the long term although it is attractive as a short term measure either for evaluating a system or to cope with heavy workloads.

Both renting and leasing costs can be written off against tax in the year they were incurred (buying involves claiming capital allowances which spreads the tax saving over several years)

Putting together a tender

It is sensible to put together a formal tender for your proposed system. This has advantages as you are able to define clearly both in your own mind and that of your supplier exactly what is required from the system.

The tender document
As a first step list the following (which are to be included as part of the tender documentation).

*   A description of your business and of its activities.

*   Details of the activities to be computerised in as much detail as practical, for example the expected volumes of data going through the system (e.g. 200 purchase invoices a week) for each activity you intend to computerise.

*   The response times required from the system, are you prepared to sit around for several minutes while the system finds the next customer record.

*   How your needs are likely to grow over the next few years.

*   The servicing and maintenance requirements you expect.

The next step is to produce a list of possible suppliers. It is best not to choose too many if only because it is likely to produce confusion, two or three is a reasonable number for most small systems

You should ask the prospective suppliers to give you the following information:

*   A description of their business.

*   The size of their organization i.e. staffing, premises and turnover.

*   The number of years experience (in this business).

*   How many systems they have installed.

*   References from clients or the phone numbers of some previous clients.

*   Training and maintenance facilities available, and (after-sales) support offered.

*   Details of the proposed systems with detailed costings.

Evaluating the suppliers' proposals

When you receive replies from the suppliers, look especially at these points:

*   Do the proposals meet your requirements.

*   Do the costs meet your budget (remember to include on-going costs such as maintenance and training).

*   Is the support offered acceptable to you.

The contract

Although the contract is the formal legal documentation that exists between the supplier and you, **all details** of the transaction should be in writing so that there is some record in case of problems.

If problems do arise, they may be able to be settled amiably, however having written documentation certainly helps to prove who is responsible for solving the problem and who pays.

It is best to buy all your system needs from the same supplier, otherwise it can be a problem proving who is actually responsible for the fault. Usually the hardware supplier will blame the software supplier and vice versa. If you have the same supplier for both this situation will not arise.

If you are at all uncertain about your legal position it is worth the money to consult a solicitor specialising in contract law (most solicitors' practices operate a special half-hour interview for a very small sum, although you must explain this is what you want when booking an appointment).

The main sections covered by the contract should be:

Systems specification
Precise details on what is to be supplied.

Hardware
The agreement to supply, deliver (and assemble) the equipment at an inclusive overall cost on a specific day and time. Also there should be details of the warranty or guarantee for the system.

Software
The licensing agreement for the programs and details on the availability and the costs of program updates.

Setting up the system
Who is responsible for getting the system running and exactly what work is to be done (e.g. are all your records to be put onto the system by the supplier). The costs of this and when it is to be finished by.

Maintenance
Details of the maintenance offered, the costs and the expected waiting time for the engineer (same day, next day, 48 hours, etc.). Also whether a loan machine is supplied.

Disclaimers
The best bit. Read this very carefully. It may exclude the seller from responsibility for almost everything.

Penalties
There may be mention of penalty clauses for late delivery (or not).

Remember that a contract is a two way affair, you are able to change or add any clauses to the contract that you (or your solicitor) wish.

In the end it is your money and your business which may suffer so make sure the contract suits you before agreeing to it.

There is consumer legislation which may make certain Clauses and conditions in the contract illegal. However to prove this will cost money and time and may ruin your relationship with your supplier.

The best way is to make sure the contract is acceptable to you before signing it.

Do not be rushed into making a decision, your business has survived until now, a few weeks or months is not going to make that much difference. A poor choice of system could however be very expensive.

Software

This chapter looks at software, firstly at DOS (disc operating systems) and then at the variety of applications programs available for businesses.

Disc operating systems

Commonly called DOS, these programs are a fundamental part of a personal computer system, they allow you and the hardware to communicate with each other.

All computer systems need an operating system although you may be protected from the DOS by the use of a menu or shell program or by the new GUI programs such as Windows 3 and not realise that DOS actually exists.

It is useful though to have an idea of what a disc operating system actually does and why every computer system needs one.

What DOS actually does

DOS controls the operation of the computer hardware while it is carrying out routine tasks such as displaying information on the screen or copying files.

The main activities of any operating system are

*   Managing the resources of the system efficiently (this includes the processor, the input devices, the output devices, the internal memory and the discs).

*   Allowing you to carry out housekeeping tasks such as formatting a disc or deleting a file.

*   Automatically handling such activities as writing files to disc and managing the disc space efficiently.

The most recent versions of DOS provide a shell (a kind of menu of commands) so that you do not have to face the complexities of the DOS prompt.

There are two major players in the PC DOS market place, Microsoft being the dominant, and Digital Research being the one that tries harder.

Microsoft DOS has gone through several versions, the currently available one being 5. Version 5 is superior in every way to the previous versions (it supports better memory management and allows disc partitions above 32Mb among other innovations).

Some suppliers are still offering the older versions and I suggest you ask for the newest version from the supplier. Version 4 is the least successful if only because it uses a lot of memory (so the application program has less space to work in and is consequently slower).

Digital Research offer DRDOS version 6. This is an excellent operating system and is increasingly being offered as a bundle with systems instead of Microsoft DOS. Certainly DRDOS seems to be slightly more innovative at present.

Really the choice between DR and MS DOS is not of importance to most users and you can be happy that whichever is included in your system will do its job effectively.

Programs that supplement DOS

There are programs available that both allow you to carry out DOS tasks more quickly, easily and efficiently and allow you to carry out certain activities DOS cannot.

General utilities

Two of the most popular are PC-Tools and Norton Utilities. These cover much the same ground although both have strengths lacking in the other (what these are depends upon your needs).

Some of the useful features offered include:

*   Testing the disc for errors, both in the disc surface and in the files.

*   Fixing errors on the discs.

*   Unerasing files and unformatting discs (where it has been done in error). Please believe me it is possible to do this by accident.

*   Creating disc caches. These are designed to speed up the transfer of information from the disc to the internal memory.

*   Defragmenting the disc. (When files are stored on the disc they are scattered all over the disc, this makes reading them slower. A fragmentation utility re-arranges the files on the disc so that all the parts of the file are stored next to each other). This can speed up access to the hard disc considerably.

*   Finding files anywhere on the disc. On a hard disc with many hundreds of files, it is wonderful to be able to locate any file quickly.

*   Setting passwords to sensitive programs or data files.

*   Viewing files. (To see the contents of the file quickly without having to load the relevant application program).

These programs have various level of use from the beginner to the expert and every competent computer user will find them invaluable.

Specific utilities

Apart from the type of programs above which are essentially collections of useful utilities and as such represent very good value for money, there exist stand alone utilities which are worthwhile if you find a need for them.

It is worth checking if the particular program you are interested in is included in either Norton or PC Tools as they contain utilities which are also available separately (it is probably much better value to buy Norton or PC Tools if this is the case).

Examples of the programs available include the following (this is in no way an exhaustive list but is intended to give you a flavour of the variety of programs on offer).

SCREEN SAVERS

These are utilities which either blank the screen or produce moving patterns and pictures. They exist to prevent screen burn-in which can happen if an image is left on the VDU screen for a period of time. Various screen saver programs are available, a very popular one is called Screen Peace. They are often included with other programs, e.g. Norton Commander.

CHECKIT.

This program is designed to tell you what exactly is wrong with your computer system, it is a diagnostic tool.

QEMM.

A very useful but somewhat specialised program that help you to set up your system memory in the most effective way. DOS operating systems allow you do the same things but with varying degrees of assistance. You do need expanded or extended memory to take advantage of this program (see Appendix 1).

XTREE.

A program that simplifies DOS housekeeping activities. An excellent option is Norton Commander which also enables you to create easy to use menu systems for your programs.

A screen showing a menu created using Norton Commander:

```
C:\>




            ---------- User Menu ----------------
            A   Works
            B   Windows
            C   Utilities
            D   dBASE 3+
            E   Sage
            F   Strategy games
            H   Education
            I   Games
            J   Qbasic
            K   Closing down the system
            -------------------------------------------
```

These programs provide a very easy to use shell with all the commands laid out in menus. If you find the original DOS command structure or DOS shell frightening then these may well be the answer.

LAPLINK.
This enables two computers to transfer files. An ideal and cheap way of transferring files from your old computer to your new if they have different size floppy disc drives. You may of course find it better to have both size floppy disc drives on your new computer and avoid the problem. This program was developed to allow portable computers to link to desktop computers but can obviously be used between two desktop systems.

STACKER and SUPERSTOR
These are interesting programs, they compress files so that they need less disc space, thereby increasing the effective size of the disc. This has become necessary with the popularity of Windows 3 programs as they use several megabytes of disc space each. All graphics programs and files need vast amounts of disc space.

Compression programs have been around for some years, the difference here is that the compression and decompression are carried out automatically without any user intervention.

The tests suggest that there is little or no time penalty in loading or storing the program and data files from or to the hard disc

These programs can save you buying a new hard disc as they can increase the effective storage area by a factor of two. Be warned though they may not be compatible with your operating system (check with your supplier before buying). DRDOS6 contains a version of SuperStor.

A word of warning, compression programs need be installed carefully and it is vital to take backups of all your files before installing the program.

I would suggest that when specifying your system you choose a Hard Disc drive size much larger than you believe necessary. This is particularly true if you are going to run Windows 3 programs as they (each) take up a considerable amount of disc space.

Believe me your disc space will fill very rapidly indeed.

Applications

In this section we are going to look at how a computer system can be used in a business. We will begin with an application that every business will need, word processing.

Word processing (WP)

WP programs have come a long way since they were glorified text editors and the range of features available approach those of a desk top publishing program.

A WP program is concerned with entering text and altering it (correcting, inserting and deleting text, moving text around the document) and formatting it or laying it out in the most effective way (setting margins, justifying, centring, using bold, italics, underlining). The document can be saved to disc, recalled, altered, printed out and saved in its new version.

In addition to the basic features mentioned above, there are some very sophisticated features which are available.

Some of the more advanced features are:

Search and replace
Searching for a word or phrase and replacing it with another (you do not realise how useful this is until you need to use it).

Mail-merging
Automatically merging a list of names and addresses with a letter (ideal for mail shots, etc.).

Spellchecking
Checking and correcting your spelling (this is of enormous benefit in PR terms, poorly spelled correspondence does not impress the reader).

Thesaurus
As in Roget (being able to select other words with similar meaning).

Repagination
Being able to decide where to begin a new page on the printer.

Running heads
Also called headers and footers, this is text which is repeated at the top or bottom of every page (e.g. the title of the chapter).

Pagenumbers
Automatic page numbering.

Footnotes
Notes at the bottom of the page indexed to text in the page explaining the indexed word.

Font control
Used in conjunction with the printer this means being able to alter the size and design of the characters being printed. You need to make sure your proposed WP program has a print driver for your printer (a print driver is a program that allows the computer and printer to communicate).

Proportional spacing
Each character is printed in a space proportional to its size, thus the letter i takes up less space than the letter w.

Calculation
Automatically adding up columns of figures.

Columns (snaking)
Displaying text in the same way as a newspaper does.

Graphics
Boxing, shading, line drawing and being able to import pictures from a paint program or other graphic format (e.g. a spreadsheet graph), so that the text and graphics can be combined in the same document.

Page preview
Also called print preview. You can see how the finished document will look before printing it out. This saves time, paper and effort and is a very useful feature.

Outlining

You can create the overall structure of the document (headings, sub headings and so on before any text is entered). The idea is that this helps with the creative process, it is most useful with longer reports and documents.

Help

The level of on-screen help varies from the simple to context sensitive help (this means help that is relevant to the current problem).

Indexing/Table of contents

Automatic generation of an index or contents list (again remarkably useful tools that you do not realise you need until you use them).

Macros

These are programs which are either supplied with the program or which you can (fairly easily) write yourself. They can be used to automate activities you want to carry out regularly.

WP programs all carry out the same kind of activities, although some are easier to use than others. The ones with least features tend to be easier to use. If you buy a cheaper (and less well featured) program make sure that it saves files in a format that can be used with a more sophisticated program if your needs develop.

Several programs offer cut down (less well featured) versions for beginners (and for use with less powerful computers) and which provide upward compatibility with the full version. The documents created using these programs can normally be used with the full version without any changes.

When buying the program make sure it will run on your specific system. If you rely on the expertise of the seller then the legal responsibility lies with them (although proving this may be troublesome).

> **Always check that the particular features you want for your work exist in your chosen WP program and that they are easy to use (some features are easier to use in some programs than others).**

Finally unless there are pressing reasons to do otherwise, buy a well known program, it is less likely to contain bugs and the support may be better. Examples of well known WP programs include Wordstar, Microsoft Word, Word Perfect and AmiPro. There are both DOS and Windows versions of these programs. Also for those of you brought up on the Amstrad PCW, there is a PC version of Locoscript available.

Desk top publishing (DTP)

DTP is the name given to low-cost publishing using a computer system to prepare material which can be used as a master copy for printing or to produce copies directly off the computer printer.

On a computer system DTP programs are used in a similar way to word processing, the document can be displayed on screen and altered as necessary. The finished result can be saved to disc or printed out as desired.

DTP programs are useful to improve the appearance of office documents and if you have material which you have typeset at present then using DTP can mean substantial cost savings, a faster product and increased control over the product.

DTP features include:

Text and graphics can be imported from the programs used to originate them. It is usually better to create the text with a WP program and the pictures with a graphics or drawing program.

The page can be viewed with both text and graphics. It can then be edited, for example a picture can be moved around the page and sized as necessary.

Different fonts (characters sizes and designs) can be used, thus headings can be in a different font to the other text.

Using boxes, lines and shading in the document is easy compared with other programs.

More advanced techniques such as kerning (controlling the space between characters), tracking (controlling the space between words) and leading (controlling the space between lines) are available.

The results can be printed out on a computer printer or used as camera-ready copy for offset-litho printing.

For professional quality either a laser printer or offset-litho gives the best results, although the new generation of ink-jet printers give almost as good a finished product as lasers at a reduced initial and running costs.

DTP is concerned with publishing, i.e. the production of printed matter, and can therefore be used for simple memos, letters, reports, brochures, magazines, pamphlets, manuals, catalogues and books.

You are limited only by your imagination, although it is fair to point out that restraint and taste should be used in the page design or the results will be extremely messy.

DTP programs have had a dramatic effect on the world of publishing, both amateur and professional. Magazines and other publications are now created entirely on desktop PC's (either as a PostScript file for direct typesetting or using the printed pages for photographing).

It is quite time consuming to learn to make the best use of DTP and if the most effective use is to be made formal training may be necessary.

DTP makes more demands on the hardware than almost any other type of program and unless the hardware is adequate you will spend too much valuable time watching the screen redraw the image rather than actually achieving anything. You should therefore buy the fastest computer system you can afford (with a large fast hard disc and plenty of RAM memory).

If you are unsure whether you need DTP now, it may be better to buy a WP program that contains some of the features of DTP (e.g. Word, Word Perfect and Wordstar, especially the Windows 3 versions) and use that.

Eventually you may find these programs limiting as WP programs are mainly text orientated and while most DTP tasks can be achieved, there is less easy control over layout. At which point you can buy a proper DTP program.

Examples of DTP programs for the PC include Ventura, Pagemaker, and Timeworks. Timeworks will work happily on a 8088/8086 processor (XT) but the others need more powerful processors e.g. a 386 with at least 4Mb of RAM to run at a reasonable speed.

Accounting systems

One of the most common reasons for a small business to buy a computer system is for accounting. There are many suitable accounting programs on the market and your accountant may well have views on which is most suitable for your needs.

There are two main types of program available:

Bookkeeping programs
These are primarily concerned with recording the transactions of the business (invoices sent and received, payments to suppliers, etc.). These may be just simple computerised cash books.

Accounting programs
These are more sophisticated and as well as recording the transactions of the business, will produce information from them (profit and loss accounts, balance sheets, aged debtors reports, etc.).

Remember that you are computerising what have been manual tasks and an accounting package works in the same way, keeping to the rules of double entry and using the same kind of structure as manual records.

The main advantages of keeping your accounts on a computer are speed, cost savings, accuracy and most importantly being able to produce useful information when it is needed.

Often you can get information from a computerised system quickly and easily that may be impossible from the manual system (for example a list of the customers owing you money analysed month by month would be a time consuming project manually but merely takes a few keystrokes on a computerised system).

The features offered by computerised accounting programs will vary both with the price and the quality of the program, as will the support offered.

Accounting programs may include the sales ledger, purchase ledger, nominal ledger, the trial balance and profit and loss account and Balance Sheet production. Other features available include invoice production, stock control, credit control facilities, VAT accounting, payroll, job costing, order processing and so on.

The cheaper accounting programs are usually integrated programs which contain the ledgers plus stock and invoicing options. Check that these programs will be able to cope with the demands of your business as although they tend to be relatively easy to use and are value for money, they may not contain all the features you need or be powerful or fast enough.

The more expensive accounting programs are made up of modules (for example a sales ledger module).

These modules can be used as stand alone programs or they can be integrated with other modules to form a suite of accounting programs.

This approach allows you to put together the modules you actually want (rather than buying a program that contains elements you will never use). For example many businesses will not need such features as multiple ledgers or multi location stock control modules.

If you are interested in the modular approach check the overall cost of all the modules you need and also check just how they are integrated (e.g. is data automatically passed from one module to another and is there a menu system to allow the modules to be easily used together).

These screens from Sage Financial Controller show the options available within a typical accounting program:

This one is the primary or main menu

```
Sage Menu Program          TESTFILES            29th February 1992




                    Sales Ledger
                    Purchase Ledger
                    Nominal Ledger
                    Payroll
                    Stock Control
                    Sales Order Processing
                    Purchase Order Processing
                    Report Generator
                    Utilities

                    Quit
```

This one is the menu for the nominal ledger.

```
Financial Controller       Nominal Ledger       29th February 1992


                    No. of entries :  0

        Nominal Account Structure     Accounts List
        Bank Transactions             Trial Balance
        Petty Cash Transactions       Transaction History
        Journal Entries               Control Account History
        Recurring Entries             Day Books
        Prepayments and Accruals      VAT Return Analysis
        Depreciation                  Monthly Accounts
        Consolidation                 Asset Valuation
        Quick Ratio
```

Questions you need to consider include the following:

*   Will the program handle the volume (number of) accounts necessary (both at present and planned for the future).

*   Is it upwardly compatible (can the data be moved to a larger, more sophisticated program without much effort or expense).

*   Will it handle the type of data you use (discounts, foreign exchange rates, invoice numbers, account codes, etc.).

*   Can standard reports be produced (can they be easily exported to a WP program for better presentation).

*   Is the program user friendly (easy enough for your staff to use), are the system manuals helpful.

*   Are there any security features built in (or do you mind anyone looking at the files).

*   Does it provide adequate audit trails of the transactions.

*   Is it fast enough (when working with the amount of data you have).

*   Can it be used on a network.

Examples of accounting packages include Sage Financial Controller, Pegasus and Sybiz Windows Accounting.

Some ideas on installing an accounting system

You should never install an accounting system without advance planning, it is not like a word processing program or a spreadsheet.

There are various ways to do this, and the following suggestions may help you plan.

It is best to install the system at the start of your financial year or at the end of a VAT period.

As a first step (before you begin to use the program live) you should install the names and other details of your suppliers, customers, stock types and other standing information.

One of the more difficult activities is setting up the Nominal Ledger and in particular the Nominal Ledger Coding structure. If you are unsure about this it is worth money to get a professional to help you. If you create a messy system it will be inefficient to use and costly to alter.

At the end of one accounting year and the beginning of the next extract the balances on all your accounts and then enter them into the new accounting system (obviously this will take a few days and may need your accountant's help).

Always run parallel systems for a period of time (this means running both the old manual and the new computerised systems side by side). This is time consuming and costly but is a necessary security procedure if things go wrong.

Remember not to be too ambitious, it may be best to begin with the sales ledger and when this is working well, then to install the purchase ledger. By this time you will be more confident and may like to computerise the Nominal Ledger and Stock and so on.

Spreadsheets

Spreadsheets are used to solve financial and other numeric problems by automating the calculations and allowing you to look at the data in various ways.

The actual program is based around cells made by a grid of rows (across) and columns (down). Text, figures or calculations (formulae) can be entered into any individual cell.

One of the attractions of spreadsheets is being able to use formulae for the calculations, having done this any change to any of the figures will be reflected in the answer (the program having been told how to calculate the answer not what the answer is, so the answer is recalculated whenever the figures are changed).

Time can be saved by being able to copy not just text or numbers into other cells but also formulae, this can also reduce mistakes.

Spreadsheets can be used to prepare reports, they can produce graphs and charts, some have database facilities and a few have simple programming languages attached.

All spreadsheets contain mathematic functions which are useful and allow the calculation of (for example) net present value and annual rate of return.

Another of the major benefits from using spreadsheets is being able to ask "What If" questions. For example if you had created a worksheet for the next years sales budgets you could then alter various figures to see what would happen in different situations. This would give you instant feedback and enable you to make more coherent and accurate decisions.

Charting
One of the most useful features of the spreadsheet is the graphing or charting facility. The graphs and charts available include pie charts, bar charts and line graphs which can be drawn from the data in the spreadsheet.

The charting feature differs from program to program in its ease of use and in the sizes and the number of items allowed in each graph (for example the number of pie charts that can be displayed together), the availability of different fonts (design and sizes of characters), and the ability to add text to the graph. The latest spreadsheet programs allow true 3-D graphics.

Reports
Some programs have built-in WP features to combine text with the figures and graphs. Others allow the graphs and figures to be exported into a WP program or DTP program and then text can be merged with the graph and figures to produce a complete report.

Advanced features
State of the art spreadsheets are 3-dimensional, this is similar to having different sections of your work on different pages, and being able to move from one page to another easily and also to be able to see more than one page at a time

Finally
As with all programs there is a balance between features, ease of use and speed. It is certainly worthwhile checking that the spreadsheet program you are interested in has facilities to import and export files from your other programs.

Examples of well known spreadsheet programs include Lotus 1-2-3 (the industry leader, Lotus is available in several current versions), Excel, Wingz, Quattro Pro and SuperCalc.

SuperCalc is an interesting program from a marketing point of view, its distributors radically reduced the price in order to sell more copies. At the time the industry were not impressed, however the gamble paid off and after-sales service has not apparently suffered. A point for the future.

Databases

Databases are used to store facts, an example of this is your customer names and addresses. These could be stored in a database file and then the file could be interrogated (looked at) in many different ways, for example listing all the customers in a certain area or those who bought a certain product from you.

Database programs are available in different levels of complexity and sophistication.

Flat-form databases
These approximate to the traditional card index file used in offices for years.

The datafile is made up of records. Each record contains data relating to a specific item, e.g. a person (similar to a card index where it was called a record card).

The ways in which data can be looked at varies with the sophistication of the program (and of the user). Other variations include facilities for checking data as it is entered and screen designs for data input.

Some database programs enable you to print reports (which allow you to lay out the data in different ways) and the reports can be incorporated into a word-processed document.

Another feature is mail-merging either within the program itself or in association with a word-processing program (this assumes your WP program can access the records in your database file, a point worth checking if this is important to you).

Relational databases

These are a more complex version of a flat form database. With these more than one database file can be used at one time and the files can be manipulated together.

These are also called hierarchical databases. The data is put together in such a way as one datafile contains master records and the records in another file can be attached to the master records.

For example a firm may decide to have two datafiles for the employees, one a personnel file (each record containing names, ages, home address etc.) and the other a salary file (each record containing name and salary details).

For security reasons these operate as separate datafiles, but in a relational structure they can be linked (if needed) by name, with the personnel file being the master file and the salary file being the slave file.

Thus an authorised person could look at both datafiles together and would be able to look at both salary details and personnel data (something other employees could not do), and could manipulate data across both files, e.g. add new data, create new fields, etc., which would update both files.

Free text databases

Certain kinds of information will not fit into the normal kind of database structure, for example the contents of a book.

Free text databases can be used with this type of data, however they do not have the same kind of features found in the other types of database program. What is offered is a search that looks for words or phrases appearing together (or close to each other), this can be useful if you are trying to find information on a certain product for example and are looking through several years' copies of a trade journal.

Menu-driven or programmable

There are two distinct approaches to the design of database programs, they can either be menu driven or programmable (with certain programs both approaches are available).

A menu-driven program presents you with a series of menus from which you choose the options wanted. Using these menus you can store data, look at the data in various ways, edit it and produce reports.

This type of program is ideal for the relatively simple application and for the non-programmer to use (for example a datafile containing customer names and addresses would be ideally suited to this type of program).

Programmable databases allow you to create very sophisticated programs and many commercial programs are written using one of these (the industry standard is the dBASE language, although this is not a task for the raw beginner unless they have plenty of time and an enquiring mind).

There are several programs which combine a menu for non-programmers with a programming language (dBASE, Dataease) giving the best of both worlds (at a price).

Other than with very simple databases, it can be a little threatening to the newcomer to set up a database so look for one which is easy to use. Do not necessarily believe the salesman.

Other points to look for are whether the program has:

*   Good reporting facilities (this means being able to print your data out as you want to see it).

*   Is easy to use (are you required to learn programming commands to actually produce anything useful)

*   Can graphs be drawn (if not can the data be exported into a spreadsheet or presentation program that can draw suitable graphs).

The hardware requirements will vary with the size of your database, the speed and size of the disc being paramount. A fast processor is also useful.

With the introduction of GUI's (graphical user interfaces) and in particular Windows 3, several database programs have been written to take advantage of this, Superbase being an example. Superbase allows you to create what looks like a piece of paper on screen complete with pictures (as can be seen from their advertisement, this lends itself to applications such as personnel records).

Examples of well known database programs include dBASE 3+, dBASE 4, Reflex, Dataease, Paradox, Superbase and Q&A.

Integrated packages

There are several integrated packages on the market. These normally contain the following modules (or sections):

Word processing
Spreadsheet (with graphs and charts)
Database

Often they will also contain a comms or communication module which allow you to communicate with other computer users via the telephone system (a modem is also required for this).

Integrated packages are aimed at the small business user who does not require the more sophisticated features found in an individual program (for example the integrated package may not allow newspaper-like columns to be produced in the WP module).

Examples of integrated packages include Lotus Works, Microsoft Works and Lotus Symphony.

Usually one or two modules within the package are stronger than the remaining (for example in Microsoft Works the WP and spreadsheet modules are quite powerful and are perfectly suited to most small and medium sized firms, however the database is less sophisticated and is only really suitable for names and address type of data).

The idea behind integrated packages is that of a low cost program suitable for most users, and where the commands within each module are similar. This means that you are not faced with radically different screens or commands for each type of activity.

Another major advantage is the ease with which items can be cut and pasted from one module to another (for example a graph produced within the spreadsheet section can be moved into the WP section and incorporated into a document). This is easier within the integrated package than by using stand-alone programs which are not integrated.

When you become more sophisticated and need to use a more powerful program then the files produced using the integrated program can usually be converted into a form that can be readily used by the new program.

Integrated programs are an excellent idea if your needs are relatively simple or if you want an easy to use program that caters for most small business needs. They are often marketed as "the only program a small business will ever need". This may well be true for you.

If you are only starting to computerise and feel that this type of program will be perfectly adequate then buy one. You can move to a more sophisticated program if necessary later (when you have had experience and know more precisely what you want the program to do). The features available in the best integrated programs are extensive and are as good as, if not better than individual programs available a few years ago.

GUI's (graphical user interfaces)

These have given a new direction to the personal computer industry. The most popular is Windows 3, which has sold several million copies in the space of a year and has been the fastest selling program ever.

A graphical interface uses pictures (called icons) instead of text. This protects you from the complexities of dealing directly with DOS (disc operating system).

When you boot up (turn the computer on) you will be presented with a screen which displays all the different application programs available to you as a series of pictures, you can then use the mouse to select one.

The screen you will be presented with will be similar to this:

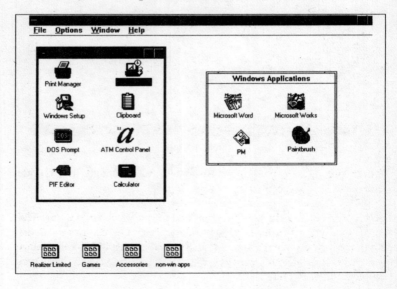

Almost all new program development taking place nowadays is for programs that can be used with Windows 3. The sheer number of copies sold and the popularity of the program means that the future of personal computing will eventually be based around this kind of GUI. Almost all the major suppliers of application programs have versions for Windows either available or for release in the very near future.

Another example of a Windows 3 screen (this time showing a pull down menu used with a word processing program):

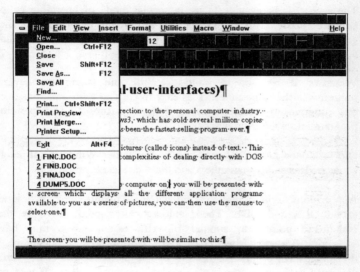

There are one or two points to think about though, if you are intending to join the Windows users.

Windows 3 is a fairly slow program and to run it you need a powerful processor and a fast hard disc (Windows programs use large amount of disc space for storage and you really need at least 80Mb of capacity on your hard disc if you are intending to use several Windows applications).

A 386SX processor with at least 2Mb of RAM is a minimum for successful use with Windows (4Mb is better). A mouse is essential for using Windows.

Although Windows 3 can be run on 80286 machines it will not be exactly fast, and there are other differences between running Windows on a 286 and 386 processor. On a 386, you can do two useful things not available on a 286.

The first is being able to run DOS programs in a window. Applications written for Windows can automatically be run as windows (so that you can have several programs on the screen at the same time).

The second is being able to use a special mode of operating called enhanced mode. This allows free disc space to be used as RAM, thus giving virtually unlimited RAM. Since disc access is slower than RAM access, there is a speed penalty.

Windows allows you to multi-task (this means running several programs at the same time). It is easy to cut and paste material from one program to another (say to copy a picture from a painting program into a word-processor).

Old fashioned DOS programs can be run under Windows (although some are less stable than others and these can cause problems).

Applications written under Windows may feature new techniques called OLE and DDE. These automatically update any file that contains a pointer to another file (for example you may have incorporated a spreadsheet chart into a word-processed document, if the spreadsheet program is used to update the chart, the chart within the word-processing file is also updated automatically). These are rather useful and can save time and effort.

Perhaps the most useful feature for the newcomer is that Windows 3 applications all have a consistent look and feel. This means that the screens look similar from program to program and the pull down menus contain similar options. Learning a new application is not the totally new experience that it could be with text based applications.

Getting Windows 3 working is relatively easy, getting it to work as efficiently as possible on your specific system requires experimentation and a certain knowledge about hardware and operating systems. If you are uncertain about this, it is a good idea to let your supplier configure the system with your chosen programs when supplying it.

However a word of warning, if you are perfectly happy with text based systems then spending money on a new system and on new software may not be particularly sensible.

As long as your system is suitable for your needs why change it.

It is possible (though unlikely) that text based systems will come back into fashion.

Finally remember that although Windows is the way forward for PC's, it is not necessarily to everyone's taste, and you may be happier with a simpler system which you use for a few tasks such as word processing and accounts.

Drawing and presentation programs

Presentation programs

These are used for producing business presentations, e.g. a marketing presentation. They are relatively simple to use and offer good control over text and some limited drawing ability.

As well as creating text and charts within the program, they can import text (from a WP program), figures and charts (from a spreadsheet) and clip-art (drawings and other art work on disc, a selection of various types of clip art can be bought from several suppliers, especially in the shareware market).

Other features include the use of templates (a predetermined layout) in order to impose a company style on the material.

Examples of this type of program include Harvard Graphics and Lotus Freelance.

Painting and drawing programs

These are easy to use but are limited in what can actually be achieved. Images can be drawn by you or scanned (using a scanner which can scan a piece of paper and store the image on a computer file), the images can then be altered in various ways, e.g. sizing, altering the colours, rotating the image and so on. Scanned images (particularly) require large amounts of RAM memory and disc space if they are be used satisfactorily.

For most people the availability of pre-drawn images (clip art) and being able to use a page scanner allow images to be used which would not be feasible if they had to be drawn (given most people's artistic ability).

The material produced from both presentation and paint programs needs to be in colour to be at its most effective for use in slide or OHP presentations. There are now various affordable colour printers on the market (both dot matrix and ink-jet printers).

Other useful programs

As well as the mainstream programs available for business purposes, there are many more specialised programs. Some of these are only available as shareware, others as commercial programs. Included in this section are some of the more interesting commercial programs.

Route finding programs
These are designed to find the quickest (or cheapest) route from one place to another. The programs allow you to specify places and roads to avoid, likely driving speeds on different types of road and to choose other preferences.

The program then calculates all the alternative routes that meet the criteria and displays them on screen, together with an estimate of the time the journey will take. A map of the routes can be displayed on screen. The information can also be printed out and stored to disc if required.

They are available for various countries and are a tremendous help in route planning (for anything more than the shortest journey). They are useful both for the salesman, the fleet manager and indeed any individual seeking a route planning aid. Examples of this type of program are Autoroute and Navigator.

Project management
These enable you to plan the most effective and efficient use of staff, materials and other business resources. For example they can be used to avoid the over stocking of an item or running out of the item. They can also be used to determine the effects of different actions on the overall business or the best way of scheduling activities.

Project management tools have been used for some years, but are only now becoming available on PC's. Two of the more reasonably priced are On Target and Superproject. These can be used for everyday planning and are relatively easy to use even by those who are not project management specialists.

Sales management programs

These are sales and marketing tools letting you maintain information about your customers and suppliers, they allow you to keep records of your sales contacts, analyse sales (and sales staff) performance and to create reports. They may also assist you in creating mailshots to potential customers and identifying new marketing and sales areas.

Program to automate activities

Much of a PC user's time is spent carrying out housekeeping chores. Programs are available which will do these while no-one is using the PC (e.g. at night). Among other activities they can make backups of the hard disc and update and print files. Two low-priced examples are Automate Anytime and Autorun.

Shareware and public domain software

This is a relatively new idea in software. It has developed from a minority activity to one which is supported by many different shareware retailers (as can be seen from the advertisements in the computer magazines). There are now magazines devoted purely to the subject.

Shareware originated from the U.S.A. and is a marketing concept. The software business tends to be dominated by organizations who spend large amounts on marketing their product, and many of the small firms and individuals writing programs have insufficient resources to do this, so they tried the novel approach of shareware. The idea appealed to many people involved in writing software (who either grew up in the 1960's or who sympathised with those ideals).

Shareware programs are distributed for the cost of the disc and any administrative costs involved (a matter of a pound or two). The person buying them is normally given a 30 day period in which to try out the software and if they want to continue to use it they register with the person who wrote the program (and pay a fee).

There are several advantages from registering, you normally get a printed manual, the latest version of the program and updates when they are issued. There is also the warm glow that comes from having a legal copy of the program and helping the program writer make a reasonable living (it is unlikely anyone writing shareware is going to become a millionaire).

Shareware is therefore software you can try before buying, this takes away the risk of paying a large sum of money for a program that is found to be less than useful. It is a major industry in the U.S.A. (where people are far more honest about registering than has been the case in the U.K.).

As many of the programs originate from the U.S.A., registering them can be a hassle (although the better shareware distributors will help with this or they may do it for you).

The variety of shareware available is enormous, from business programs to games and cooking. One of the most useful areas is that of utilities (these programs are often too small and uneconomic to retail commercially). The quality though can vary from the first class to the virtually unusable.

Business programs make up a very large segment of the shareware market, be warned however that many are written for the American market.

Everything from a full featured word processing program, database or spreadsheet is available as are more specialised programs such as form design. Many of these programs are of commercial quality and provide a cheap option to the more expensive commercial programs (even after paying the registration fee). There is even a British accounting program called Page which is similar to its commercial equivalent (Sage).

After-sales support can be as good (or bad) as the commercial versions and you are certainly more likely to be talking to the person who wrote the program rather than a sales support person.

However it is expected that you will have a reasonable grasp of the use of a computer and especially of DOS (disc operating systems), this is changing though. The magazines (especially those devoted to shareware) grade the programs and this will give you some indication of their quality and ease of use.

Shareware is available from firms who advertise in the computer press and also it can be downloaded from a bulletin board (although this introduces more possibility of viruses). Most of the firms are reputable, however some are not and to be safe, use one that belongs to a professional organization, e.g. The Association of Shareware Professionals.

Public Domain software is slightly different. It is offered by the same firms distributing shareware, and is also available from bulletin boards, but it has been given to the public domain by the author who does not expect any payment for it (or for you to register it).

The best way of learning more about this fascinating subject is to buy some of the magazines devoted to it. You will have fun and may save yourself money. Shareware and Public Domain program libraries may even contain that elusive program you needed but could not find commercially (or did not know even existed).

Hardware

In this chapter we are going to look at the hardware which forms the basis of every system, i.e. the processor, the discs, the display and the printer.

The processor

The choice of processor will be determined by money and exactly what you need the system to do. Looking at the options in order of sophistication.

8088/8086
The original processors, now suffering from a lack of speed and RAM (memory). They are still useful for word processing and other simple tasks, but to run a large customer database will slow the machine down to a tortoise like pace. In fact even spell checking can be slow on these machines.

They are no longer offered by most manufacturers and if you really want one they can be bought very cheaply. It is interesting that of the major manufacturers only Amstrad are still making them (and this model is intended for home use).

80286
80286 processors are capable of operating at a faster speed then 8088/8086 machines and hence are more capable of dealing with large modern programs. They are the basic entry level machine but are now starting to be superseded in this role by the 80386SX.

They are not able to multi-task (carry out two or more activities at once). They will also run programs slower than a more advanced machine. However if all you intend to do is word-processing or accounts then these machines may well suit you.

80386

They are faster and more powerful (but slightly more expensive) and are useful for applications requiring speed for example Windows 3 which is a relatively slow program to run.

These are starting to be the entry level business machine for all but the simplest tasks and are only a little more expensive than the 80286.

They also have the advantage of being future proofed (to some extent). The reason for this is that they use a 32 bit processor and programs are beginning to be written to take advantage of the 80386 processor (and which may not work on the 80286 or lesser machines).

There are two versions of the 80386, the SX and the DX, the SX being cheaper and slower (the difference being the speed with which data is moved around internally). Both versions will run the software now being written specifically for the 80386 chip.

80386 machines have inherent advantages besides speed, they support what is known as virtual 8086 mode. This allows the processor to multi-task DOS applications. The chip can also treat hard disc space as though it is RAM memory thus giving effectively limitless RAM (there will be a penalty in speed however).

Definitely the processor to go for in terms of the future and if you are going to be doing anything other than relatively simple tasks.

80486

The newest processor, useful for, e.g. CAD (computer aided design) and for use as file servers in networks   Very fast and sexy but over the top for most purposes.

Processor speeds

Each type of processor comes in a variety of speeds (e.g. the 80286 is available from 10MHz to 20 MHz). The speed varies with the cost and it is well worth paying a little extra to get a faster machine as it will affect the speed of all your applications.

> The overall speed of the system will depend on the processor speed and that of the hard disc and it would be less than sensible to buy a very fast processor and a slow low capacity hard disc, so getting the balance right is important.

Add-on processors

Processors can have add-on maths processors for number crunching, e.g. 8087, 80387. These enable numeric calculations to be carried out much faster and allows the main processor to be used for other tasks. However the program has to be able to use them (check this before buying one).

Memory

A computer system contains internal memory called RAM and ROM (random access memory and read only memory). The important one is RAM as that is where the programs and data are stored while being processed.

The RAM capacity is expressed as Kbytes (kilobytes) or Mbytes (megabytes). 8088/8086 processors normally have 640K RAM and 80286/80386 processors have 1Mbyte RAM as standard.

With the arrival of memory hungry programs such as Windows 3, there is a need for more RAM. Unfortunately due to a design limitation DOS can only use 640K so a way around this problem was needed if large programs could be run on PCs.

The answer to this is to use extended or expanded memory (see Appendix 1) in addition to the base 640K. This is why the more powerful machines are sold with 2 or 4Mbytes of RAM, the additional memory is configured as extended (sometimes expanded) memory.

Cache memory

A system of cache memory can be used to speed up the system. The cache size is typically 16Kb to 64Kb and its purpose is to hold a copy of frequently used program code and data.

Cache memory is based on the idea that once a memory location has been accessed, it is likely to be accessed again. This means that after the initial access, later accesses need go only to the cache.

Since much computer processing is repetitive, a high hit rate in the cache can be expected. Systems using cache memory can achieve an 85 to 90 per cent hit rate. System performance can be radically improved beyond that possible with systems using the same processor but without a cache.

CMOS RAM

This type of memory is used to store setup instructions and to store other data that needs to be retained in the computer's memory, e.g. system date and time.

It is powered by an internal battery and retains its contents between sessions (until of course the battery runs down). For this reason it is vital that a copy of the setup details is kept elsewhere (e.g. written down in the system manual).

A note (or two)

Interestingly the latest survey figures show that most small businesses are using 8088/8086 and 80286 machines and have not yet made the move to the more powerful processors. If it works why change it.

Most suppliers expect systems only to be kept for three years (average) and then upgraded to the newest technology.

Do not be misled by the media or advertising hype into believing that the newest technology is necessary for you or your business.

Discs

Micro computers normally have at least one floppy disc drive and one hard disc drive.

It is necessary to have a floppy disc drive for the initial installation of the software onto the hard disc and for backing-up the files.

Formatting of floppy discs
All new discs require formatting. Different types of machine format discs differently, however the IBM standard is now commonplace.

When formatted, a disc is divided into concentric tracks and these tracks are subdivided into sectors. Formatting divides the disc electromagnetically into these sectors (sections), and labels each sector so that DOS can find the information stored on the disc.

Disc formats
This is an area where there used to be many compatibility problems. There are two current sizes of floppy discs, 5.25" and 3.5". All IBM clones use one of the IBM floppy disc formats

IBM formats

double density format
The usual size used to be a 5.25" floppy disc, double density disc which could hold 360Kbytes

However this has been replaced as the standard by the 3.5" floppy disc holding 720Kbytes.

High density formats
Again there are two sizes, firstly the 5.25" floppy disc, double sided, high density disc. This will hold 1.2Mbytes. (A 1.2Mbyte drive will read a 360Kbyte disc but if the 360K disc is recorded onto using the 1.2Mb drive, it may not be able to be read by a 360K drive).

Increasingly the standard is now the 3.5" floppy disc holding 1.44Mbytes. (A 3.5" double density disc can be used in a high density drive but not visa versa).

The different formats are important if you have several different machines with different format drives. You will normally only find older machines having a 5.25" disc drive (as its only drive). Many computers are offered with both sized drives so that both sizes of disc can be accommodated.

Hard discs

These are made of metal, and revolve much faster than floppy drives which is why data access times are much quicker. The access speed for hard discs is normally quoted in advertisements, the larger the capacity of the disc, generally the faster the access.

Nowadays a 28ms access time is relatively slow and the newer drives are quoting times of less than 20ms, some lower than 15ms. All things being equal, go for a fast access time especially if you are going to use graphic programs such as Windows 3 which will make considerable use of the disc.

Capacity of hard discs

Standard sizes for business machines start at 40MB and increase to several hundred. It is becoming noticeable that the standard 40MB disc is no longer sufficient for the newer type of programs (Windows 3, etc.) that require several megabytes of storage each and create large datafiles which also require large storage areas. You should be thinking in terms of an absolute minimum of a 50MB hard disc drive if you are intending to run Windows 3 programs and preferably an 80+MB drive.

A note when using hard discs

Before moving a hard disc machine check the procedure for disc parking which usually involves running a special program to park the heads so that they do not crash onto the disc causing incurable damage. However modern hard discs often feature auto parking which does away with the problem.

Disc caching

This is similar to RAM memory caches and improves the rate at which data can be retrieved from the hard disc by keeping a portion of data in a cache. A disc cache is used because the speed of accessing data from the disc is slow relative to the speed of the processor.

There are two methods of caching:

* Software caching uses a portion of RAM as a cache, for example, with 640Kb of RAM, 32Kb may be used for the disc cache. Better still you can use extended memory for the cache.

* Using a caching controller card which is built into an expansion slot inside the system unit. It has its own cache memory so that the full amount of RAM remains available.

It is a debatable whether hardware caches or software caches are actually the most effective, it may well depend upon your other system resources and the programs you are running. However some form of disc cache speeds the system up considerably.

Monitor specifications

To display images you need both a monitor and a video display card (which contains the electronics to drive the monitor). There are several standards of display card, however the only two that really matter are Hercules (MGA) and VGA.

Hercules (mono graphics adaptor)

The original green screen. This was the first adaptor to display graphics which it does in two colours. This is a high quality display (especially for text) and its major drawback (besides not being colour) is that there are few games which work with it.

Almost all major programs will work with this adaptor (although check this for your chosen programs) and it is a very cheap option. Some suppliers offer this as a choice, although it must be getting to the end of its useful life.

If you do go for this, remember that to upgrade to VGA will require both a new monitor and a new display card.

VGA (video graphics adaptor)

The latest standard, it is the normal choice for all systems, the only criteria being the amount of memory on the adaptor card which will affect the speed and number of colours that can be displayed at different resolutions (see Appendix 2).

The monitor

A monitor is normally included with the system and the monitor offered may well make the difference between choosing one system and another.

There are certain things to take into account with monitors:

Mono or colour
Firstly do you want colour or mono. The choice may be determined by cost and given the choice always go for a more powerful processor or larger hard disc drive as a colour monitor can easily be added later (just buy one and plug it in).

However given sufficient funds a colour display is great, many programs take advantage of a colour display (in fact it is sometimes difficult to see some messages on a mono screen). Colour screens also make a considerable difference to games (of course your staff won't have time to play games).

The dot pitch of the screen
A screen is made up of thousands of dots (or pixels) and the space between the dots varies (usually from 0.51 to 0.28mm). The higher the number the coarser the image, some screens have a very grainy appearance which can be tiring.

The resolution
The VGA standard is 640 x 480, however most monitors will display 800 x 600 (EVGA) and some 1024 x 768 (SVGA). It is worth noting that to display the highest resolution really needs a non-interlaced monitor otherwise the display is likely to flicker (although in reality using a 1024 x 768 display on a 14" monitor needs extremely good eyesight).

Interlaced and non-interlaced monitors
The difference between interlaced and non-interlaced screens is that with non-interlaced screens, the electron beam producing the image completes each line and then moves onto the next. This is faster than interlaced screens where the electron beam draws each alternate line and interlaced screens may flicker more.

The advantage of using a higher resolution display is simply that more data and programs can be displayed on the screen at the same time. Higher resolutions also enable you to display full pages of a DTP program in a readable font and are also useful to see large areas of a spreadsheet at one time.

If you want to use higher resolutions (than 640 x 480) then you may need a larger display screen than the normal 14" one. This is especially true if you are using applications that have to be looked at closely for long periods of time, for example I find word processing files easier to read and edit at 640 x 480 than at 800 x 600 (this may of course be a factor of my age or eyesight though).

If you are intending to use your machines for DTP or graphics work for extended periods then consider using a 15" or larger monitor.

> Please note that the terms EVGA and SVGA are not standard definitions and can mean different things to different suppliers (check exactly what resolution is meant).

At present only some programs can take advantage of the higher resolutions (examples being Windows 3 and Word Perfect 5.1).

Expansion

You may need to expand your system in the future (for example to install a modem or additional disc controller).

To make sure this is possible, check the space inside the casing and the number of expansion slots that can actually be used.

Desk-tops v. portables

Until recently the only viable choice was a desk-top system. These are still the normal choice and have been getting smaller but are still far from portable. However you may like to consider the idea of a portable computer either as your main machine or as a second machine to use at home or when travelling.

Portables tend to cost more than the equivalent desk-tops and are relatively less powerful with slower and smaller hard discs. Recently colour screens for portables have become available but are still rather expensive.

You should look for a backlit VGA screen with (preferably) 32 levels of grey. Memory expansion can be far more costly than for a desk-top and some portables have very limited space or potential for expansion (for example you may want to install a modem card in your portable). Remember that to run Windows 3 successfully needs a fairly powerful machine and a mouse (using one may be a problem on a crowded train though).

Portables are usually divided into three categories (although the definitions are far from rigid)

*   The laptop which is large, reasonably heavy and may be mains only.

*   The palmtop which is very small but limited in what they can do in their present state.

*   The notebook is about the size of A4 paper and fits into a briefcase. This is the strongest area of the market at present and you can buy machines to run Windows 3 with large hard discs.

When purchasing a portable check the screen display carefully as it may not be ideal in all lighting conditions. Other areas to check include the keyboard (size, number of keys and action), the build quality, the strength of the construction and the shape and size of the power supply (if external to the machine).

Battery life may be an important consideration (find out the recharging time and whether the machine can be used while recharging). Many machines have a sleep/resume feature which allows the machine to be shut and reopened and the application to be picked up at exactly the same point as before (without actually closing down the system and then starting it up again).

Some of the current market leaders are Compaq and Toshiba.

Printers

The most common types of printer are:

Dot-matrix
These form characters from a matrix of dots produced by pins in the print head hitting the ribbon and paper (different combinations of the pins produce different characters).

The number of pins affects the print quality, e.g. a 9 pin head is adequate for draft work and a 24 pin head will offer high quality (although a 9 pin printer operating in a Near Letter Quality mode will produce a reasonably legible type very slowly).

The speed of the printer is measured in c.p.s (characters per second), draft may be 160 c.p.s. and NLQ 35 c.p.s. though there is considerable variation (dependant upon price).

Most packages support a number of (popular) printers and emulations, the most common being an Epson emulation. This means that even if the program does not mention your printer by name you may still be able to use the printer successfully if it emulates the Epson standard.

Matrix printers handle a wide range of paper sizes and types (including labels). Paper is fed by a tractor mechanism (continuous stationery) or by friction (single sheets). Some dot-matrix printers can print in colour and this is increasingly being offered as an option.

It is possible to buy a single sheet feeder to automatically feed single sheets and this is best for business purposes as the paper is usually of a better quality and it is easier to use than continuous stationery.

The problems associated with impact printers are those of noise and dirt. They can produce multiple copies and cut stencils, however they may not print landscape (across the page rather than portrait which is down the page).

Dot matrix printers come in two widths, 80 column (normally) and 132 column (useful for spreadsheets and financial printouts). Many manufacturers offer matrix printers among them Citizen and Star.

Inkjet printers

These spray a high-speed stream of electronically charged drops from nozzles which create dots in a matrix form and produce colour or black and white of excellent quality. Inkjet printers are sometimes called bubblejet printers.

This type of printer has become very popular recently as the newest models combine extremely high quality with relatively low initial and running costs.

They are fairly quick, 4 ppm (pages per minute) being common. Both Hewlett Packard (HP), Olivetti and Canon make inkjet printers. The Canon BJ printer is portable and maybe a useful addition to a portable computer.

Laser printers

These combine electro-photographic printing (as in photocopiers) with high intensity lasers. They offer speed and extremely high quality print and handle graphics easily and quickly.

Makes include Hewlett Packard (HP LaserJet) and this is the industry standard so if you buy another make ensure it will emulate the HP printer codes. They cannot however be used with normal NCR multi-part stationery.

Printing speed is fast especially on multiple copies, the speeds range from 6 pages/minute to 26 ppm.

A note about print buffers

A buffer is a temporary storage area. It is necessary because input and output activities are slower than processor activities. For example data from the processor is placed in the buffer and the printer then prints out at its own speed, the data in the buffer is replaced when necessary.

This means the processor is freed to carry out other activities while the printer is working. All printers have a buffer, the size varies considerably from printer to printer and the size of the buffer may be a factor to take into account (otherwise you could be waiting for the printer to finish and be unable to use your computer).

Other interesting hardware

Worth considering are:

Scanners
A scanner allows you to capture an image on paper and store it on disc and then incorporate it into a document. The image may be a picture, a photograph, a drawing or even text.

There are two types of scanner, a hand scanner and a flatbed scanner. For normal purposes, a flatbed scanner is far more suitable and effective. Scanners vary in the quality of image they produce (get one capable of 300 dots per inch) and whether they produce a colour or mono (black and white) image.

You will need an interface card (and a spare expansion slot to fit it into). You also need to check that the format the image is saved in will be compatible with the software you are using to produce the document. Also remember that scanned images need considerable amounts of disc space.

CD Rom
These are similar (though not identical to) the CD players found in domestic hi-fi systems. They are connected to a PC and are used to store vast amounts of data which can then be read into the processor as necessary (each compact disc holds far more data than any hard disc is capable of, up to 700Mb per disc).

CDs cannot be written to, they are a medium for distributing both data and programs in huge quantities, cheaply and effectively (although each CD is expensive, if you calculate the value of the information or the number of floppy discs that would otherwise be necessary, it works out as a cheap medium).

The kind of material finding its way onto CD at present is mainly reference material, encyclopaedias and back issues of newspapers.

Unless you find an immediate need for a CD Rom, it may be worth waiting a few years until hardware prices are lower and there is more variety of content and the cost is less.

Ergonomics

Ergonomics is concerned with how design can affect the efficiency and the happiness of you and your employees.

As the number of computer users has increased, so has the emphasis on ergonomic design in the office. This is because if computer systems and the office environment are not adequately designed, users suffer from fatigue and boredom. This is especially true of the non-obsessives, e.g. clerks, accounts staff, managers, etc.

Ergonomic aspects of design

When purchasing computer equipment and furniture look at the following areas of the design:

What is the equipment to be used for
Is it to be used for entering data from documents (copytyping, entering invoices), or answering customer enquiries, or copytyping or any other tasks.

Chair height and design
If the desk is fixed in height then you need an adjustable height chair so that different people can use it. A footrest is also useful since if feet are not supported properly the blood circulation in the legs may be affected by pressure from the edge of the chair and may result in cramp.

Desks
Generally the larger working area the better. If copying work is carried out, a document holder (placed between the keyboard and the VDU) helps. Also a matt surface helps to avoid screen reflection.

Lighting
You should try to create a balance between natural and artificial light, natural lighting may not be best in every situation.

The monitor
Both the quality (of the display) and its position need to be considered, the display should be able to swivel and tilt and to be far enough away from you for comfortable viewing.

The monitor should have brightness/contrast controls which should be easy to access. You should try to avoid glare or reflections as these make the screen difficult to read. Screen filters can be used to cut out glare. You can avoid reflections on the screen by using window blinds and matt work surfaces.

Radiation
The dangers of working with VDU's include radiation emissions (these are potentially dangerous, but the radiation becomes weaker as it travels).

This is of concern (especially) to woman and children and personally I would prefer to be on the safe side and choose a low radiation monitor conforming to the EEC and Swedish regulations.

These are becoming more easily available and are now supplied as standard by some manufacturers. It is also possible to buy them separately (Philips and Taxan produce them). It seems that mono monitors may have a lower emission rate than colour ones.

Ions
There may be a lack of ions in the air around the VDU due to the high positive charge from the tube. It may help computer users to have ionisers located in the room.

Keyboards
These should be detachable and heavy enough to avoid them sliding around the desk. There should have retractable feet to allow angling to get the best typing position. Key pressure should be light and positive (perhaps with click/tactile feedback, although this may be irritating to some people).

Storage
There should be sufficient room for personal items (handbags, etc.) and work items (discs, manuals, printouts). Boxes and trolleys can be purchased for additional storage (but remember they have to be put somewhere).

Cabling
Cabling is necessary for electrical connections and for communications (networks). Loose cables should be carried through special channels in the furniture. Cable bridge conduit is designed to channel the cables safely across floors (so people do not trip over them and hurt themselves).

Flooring
Carpets are better than tiles (which tend to come unstuck), they are quieter and feel more comfortable. Woollen carpets produce less static than synthetic carpets and are therefore a better buy.

Designing the office layout
Discuss alternative layouts with the users as they will make useful contributions and will appreciate being consulted.

Try to avoid any staff working in areas of extreme temperatures (too near to radiators, draughts, etc.). Overheating can cause computer malfunctions and direct sunlight causes glare. Printers can be noisy (you can use acoustic screens/hoods or site them in another room, remember laser and inkjet printers are more or less silent in operation).

Staff have to move around so leave adequate space for this, no-one likes to work in cramped conditions.

Fires can happen, so make sure there is quick and easy access to fire extinguishers and exits. Make sure that there are sufficient working fire extinguishers, and all staff are familiar with an approved fire drill and evacuation procedure.

Colour schemes
Research has shown that it is important to choose the right colour for lighting and the working areas. Red and orange give a warm feeling, green and blue make you feel cool. Purple shocks and stimulates (and should therefore be avoided by most people). This may seem nonsense but does have a real effect on people's lives and emotions.

Noise levels
Noise can be tiring, and its effects can range from annoying to dangerous.

Irritability (a sign of strain) often results from long periods of noise (for example sitting next to a noisy dot matrix printer for hours on end may not be a problem for short periods of time, but the stress will build up).

Breaks
It is also suggested that operatives have a break every hour. This should increase their overall efficiency and work rate and make them happier and more content and productive employees.

Medical problems

The following complaints are associated with the use of computers (although there is disagreement about whether these can be attributed directly to the use of computer equipment).

General aches and pains
Headaches, sickness, eyestrain, tiredness, neck and backache, arm and wrist aches. These can be caused by screen and display quality, lighting, temperature, humidity, noise, seating position, etc.

Stress
Both psychological and physical stress can be caused by uncomfortable working positions and conditions. Shift work can also cause stress.

Eyesight problems
These can be caused by the use of contact lenses, bifocals and the side effects of certain drugs.

RSI and tenosynovitus
Thought to be caused by badly designed keyboards, bad posture and inadequate breaks in work routine. (RSI means repetitive strain injury). Employees suffering from RSI have now begun to successfully sue their employers.

Others problems

These may include damage to hearing caused by exposure to loud printers, epilepsy caused by flickering monitors, cancer caused by exposure to radiation. Miscarriages may possibly result from the radiation from monitors as can male problems which may include loss of sex drive and sterility.

Low radiation monitors may reduce these problems. It must be noted that the actual causes of these complaints are the subject of scientific controversy and speculation at present.

Electric shocks can be caused by poor wiring, overloaded sockets and the build up of static. Sprained/broken limbs can be caused by tripping over cabling and burns can result from electrical short circuits, over-heated equipment and fires.

The legal issues (health and safety)

If the foregoing hasn't put you off the whole idea then you should be aware of the legislation governing this area.

Health and Safety at work is governed by the Health and Safety at Work Act 1974, another important act that has implications for computer users is the Offices, Shops and Railways Act 1963.

There are also EEC directives on the minimum health and safety requirements for working with visual display units. Member states (e.g. the UK) should have implemented these by the end of 1992. The legislation covers (among other items) visual display units, keyboards, seating and desk surfaces as well as lighting, heating, humidity and radiation emissions.

This new legislation may have serious implications for the buyer and user of computer systems as well as the manufacturer, although it seems likely that while equipment bought after the end of 1992 will have to comply, equipment purchased before that date will be able to be used for four years before having to be updated (although your workforce may not be too impressed with using out of date and possibly unsafe equipment).

You need also to be aware of the Data Protection Act (see the section on the Law).

Networks

Computers can talk to each other by using direct links, by using local area networks (LANS) or via telephone lines.

Direct links

In its simplest form this means connecting one computer to another by making the receiving machine take its information from the serial port at the back of the computer, rather than from the keyboard, the two computers being connected by a cable.

LANs

This means two or more computers (within the same limited area) connected by cables.

Some of the reasons to have a LAN are:

*   Sharing programs and data between machines (n.b. applications programs are cheaper per unit by purchasing a network licence than by purchasing individual copies).

*   Sharing resources such as laser printers.

*   Communicating between machines and being able to share information, e.g. the customer database.

How LANs are constructed

The central feature is normally a powerful microcomputer (normally a 386 or 486 processor). The controlling micro (the file-server) requires a high capacity hard disc (to hold the programs and the data files for all the network stations).

The server also accepts jobs from the workstations for printing and the network software automatically spools all print jobs into a queue (spooling means to copy the files waiting printing onto an area of the hard disc while they wait for the printer to be ready).

Each workstation may require a network card which plugs into one of the free expansion slots inside each machine. You may also need a network operating system to control the operation of the LAN.

The cabling connecting the machines may be simple two-core twisted wire or it may be more complex. The type of LAN being installed determines the cabling.

Email

Electronic mail is another feature of networks, individuals can send and receive messages and it has many advantages over phones (telephones only operate in real time, they interrupt other conversations, create noise and irritation).

Email can operate at any time, the message waits for the recipient to log onto their terminal. When received the message can be read, edited, printed, stored or even answered. Email is also faster than either internal or external post, and by using passwords it can be made confidential.

Email thus has several major advantages over the traditional office mailing system:

*   Mail can be automatically sent, received and stored.

*   Security levels can be set (so that only the intended person will be able to read the message)

*   When you look at your mail, you can sort it by sender or by topic.

*   Mail can either be dealt with immediately, stored or deleted from the system.

*   Multiple copies of a message can be sent, i.e. the same information can be sent to several users at the same time.

Sharing information

This is a considerable benefit of networks as once datafiles are shared on a network then any user can access them and alter them. This can have problems since not every user should be allowed to alter records, also two people may try to update a record at the same time.

However most network software solves these problems by:

*   Using passwords to limit access to files or areas of the network. Some network software gives each user certain rights over the system, these may be restrict the user to only reading files, or not allowing them to create new files or alter files.

*   Record Locking, this means that if a particular record is being updated then it is locked and cannot be accessed until the updating is finished.

LAN architecture

Make sure your chosen LAN can be expanded for new users and new peripherals. You may also want to connect it to other LANs.

Using discless workstations

Most networks have floppy disc-drives built into the workstation, however workstations are available without them, and these have several advantages:

*   Security against theft of data and against viruses (no floppy disc drive, therefore there is no possibility of software being copied, data being stolen or of the introduction of viruses).

*   Reduced size and cost of the workstation, this can be important where space or money is scarce.

*   All data (and programs) are held on the server, so backup can be carried out regularly by the network manager.

However certain problems can arise with LANs. These can include system failures which can be due to hardware or software incompatibility (some application software does not run successfully on a network or may not allow the sharing of data files).

Buying a network

Unless you are technically experienced, I would suggest getting advice from your dealer as networks are more complex to set up than stand-alone systems. Many dealers are specialists in networks.

Nowadays micro-computer based networks are available in several forms:

Starter kits
These are aimed at the smaller network system and at the non-specialised user. They contain all the necessary items (manuals, cables, network cards, connectors, etc.) even including the computers themselves.

These are often called Ethernet kits or Ethernet networks (this refers to the topology or design of the network). These kits do not normally require a dedicated server so all the computers in the network can be used as workstations.

You can buy a kit and have the network running quite quickly and if any problems arise there is normally a technical hotline support available at the end of the phone. Bear in mind that these kits still require a certain level of computer expertise if they are to be installed successfully.

Their advantage is being able to try out networking, perhaps just to share a laser printer. If this is successful then it can be expanded. They are marketed by among others Sage and Novell.

The next step
At some point you may wish to expand your network beyond the capability of the starter kit. At this point you need a network which uses a dedicated file server and possibly a dedicated print server as well. You will also need to purchase a network operating system.

Microcomputer network operating system are marketed by Microsoft (LAN Manager), Novell (NETware) and Banyan (VINES).

A final note on networks
Always make someone responsible for the network by appointing a proper network manager.

Communications

WANs

The term WAN (wide area network) is used to describe the linking of computers in distant locations.

To do this requires a modem at each end to translate the computer language into a form that can be transmitted along the telephone lines and another to translate it back at the other end. Comms (communications) software is also needed to control the whole process.

By using modems (modulator / demodulator), both networks and indeed stand-alone PC's can communicate to computers around the world via the telephone system (the telephone system being a gateway to the outside).

A further benefit of using a modem is being able to extract information from commercial databases, e.g. Prestel in the U.K. and many others worldwide. This can be expensive as some of these services charge an annual subscription and the connect time is often costly.

Modem types

These are plugged into the standard telephone jack socket. Modems can have features such as auto-dial and auto-answer.

Modems can be fitted on an expansion card fitted inside the computer case or can be free-standing, and should be Hayes compatible.

They are classified by their transfer rate, the speeds are quoted in bps (bits per second)

The present transfer standards are:

Standard	Receive Speed (bps)	Transmit Speed (bps)
V21	300	300
V22	1200	1200
V22bis	2400	2400
V32	9600	9600
V32bis	14400	14400
V23	1200	75

Fax (facsimile transmission)

This involves the transmission of exact copies of the original document (a kind of photocopying over public telephone lines).

There are PC Fax systems available which allow you to send faxes from your computer system without them having to be printed out first. This means that you do not need a fax machine yourself (although obviously you cannot receive faxes unless you do). Some modems are available which double as PC Fax systems.

Bulletin boards

These are available throughout the world and cover every conceivable topic where enthusiasts are able to leave messages and communicate via the bulletin boards. They are often free but there is still the telephone connection charge to consider (especially for connections to bulletin boards abroad).

Messages and questions can be left on the bulletin board and the replies looked at some time later. Bulletin boards are a good source of public domain programs and shareware (and viruses so be careful and check any files you download with a virus checking program before using them).

Since these boards are usually operate on a 24 hour day, telephone calls can be timed for cheap period rates.

The bulletin board operator is called the system operator or sysop (who traditionally uses a pseudonym), normally the sysop is an enthusiast and most BB's are of a non-commercial nature.

Communicating with other systems

You may also want to communicate with computers in other areas of the country or even worldwide.

One of the systems that enable you to do this is Telecom Gold. This is run by British Telecom, and works on the basis of each subscriber being issued a (unique) mailbox number.

When a message is sent, it is transmitted to the mailbox number (together with a subject heading). The message is received at the other end and the subject heading is displayed on the screen.

Messages can be dealt with immediately or stored for future use. Stored messages can be looked at by using keywords (e.g. subject) and the system allows for confirmation of receipt and the use of passwords to maintain confidentiality.

Using Telecom Gold or similar systems is cheaper and quicker than the telephone and there is evidence of the communication taking place. It also avoids the time wasted trying to get through on the telephone.

It is also faster and more reliable than the postal services, and messages can be sent at any time. It is possible to send telexes (even though the sender does not have a telex service) via Telecom Gold.

Prestel

This is a public system providing hundreds of thousands of pages of information placed on the system by organizations (called information providers). It is the English Viewdata system.

The information is continuously updated and covers many areas from the financial sector through other business information to leisure pursuits.

You can access this information by using a modem and the normal telephone system. You do have to pay a subscription to Prestel, a connect charge and also pay for certain of the information provided (most of the information pages are free, the costly ones tend to provide up to the minute financial information).

Prestel is interactive, this means that you can order goods and services through the system and can leave messages for the information providers. It can also be a vehicle for electronic mail.

When you subscribe to the system you are given a directory of the information providers and a password. To use Prestel you dial up the system and enter your identity / password. You are then presented with a series of menus to allow you to access the information you want.

CUGs
Some of the Prestel pages are restricted to the members of CUGs (closed user groups). These are groups of people with common interests and where the information provider wishes to restrict access to the data they are providing.

Private viewdata systems
These are created by organizations to provide their employees and customers with information specific to their firm. Some of these are linked to the public viewdata system (Prestel) and can be accessed by outsiders. The travel industry make considerable use of private viewdata systems as can be seen in any travel agents.

Gateways

This is a term which means allowing users access to other viewdata systems via Prestel (for example access into a private viewdata system).

Services offered by the Prestel system

Prestel travel offers information on public travel services, timetables and fares and you can book tickets directly. Home banking services are offered so you can organize your finances electronically.

Prestel offers information from the world's financial centres, stock prices, exchange rates and general business news and updates. There is an electronic version of the Yellow Pages.

You can use a mailbox facility within Prestel to send messages to other Prestel users and there is a Telex link whereby telexes can be sent.

Prestel can also provide a gateway to various external databases which provide archive material (for example various publications have put their back material onto computer database).

Security

How to keep all your precious files and systems safe

Computer security is a subject much discussed but often not carried out.

Although carrying out security procedures may be time consuming, the chaos caused by the loss of all or parts of your data is far more expensive both in time and money.

The effects of damage to the system can include:

* Financial losses caused by the disruption

* Loss of staff morale

* Loss of customer and supplier goodwill

* Failure to meet legal requirements (e.g. VAT returns)

Remember that

The best security procedure is of no practical use unless it is carried out.

The main causes of damage

Fire

This does not happen often, but if it does the results can be traumatic. Even small fires can have an appalling affect on computer systems (for example a lit cigarette accidentally thrown into a waste bin next to the computer or printer).

Apart from being careful, there are some positive steps that can be taken to minimise the results of a fire.

*   Always keep your backup discs in a fireproof cabinet away from the computer itself.

*   Have fire alarms fitted and kept in working condition (the alarms should detect smoke as well as fire, as smoke can cause more damage than the fire itself). Fire extinguishers should be kept in a working state. There are several different types of fire extinguisher some of which are slightly less damaging to computer equipment (and to humans).

*   Fire resistant partitioning can be used to slow the spread of fire.

Water (flooding)

The likelihood of this will depend on your location, however plumbing and central heating systems have been known to flood. The only suggestions here are keeping backups somewhere else and keeping the equipment off the floor.

Illegal acts

This covers fraud, sabotage, arson, hacking, etc. The answer here is to prevent access to the system, which can be achieved in the following ways:

*   Keep the system in a locked room.

*   Employ guards and dogs (this may seem somewhat extreme for a small business).

*   Use some form of password control to prevent undesirables using the system (this is also a useful technique to avoid staff having access to sensitive files, for example the payroll data files).

Passwords

Passwords can apply to the whole system (to use the system a password has to be entered at the keyboard) or they can apply only to certain files (e.g. payroll files).

To be effective passwords have to work. They should:

*   Be unique to each user.

*   Not easily guessed (wife's name, dogs name, initials).

*   Changed regularly.

*   Not written down.

*   Not given to anyone else (**for any reason**).

> Unfortunately the research that has been carried out shows that most passwords are far too easy to find out or guess and users tend to treat them as a kind of joke.

Mechanical problems

These can cause the computer to break down, causing damage to the datafiles. The most likely scenario is a disc crash where the disc is physically damaged. This can happen at any time and the safety measures are to take regular backups of data and a maintenance contract so that the problem can be fixed quickly and cheaply.

Software problems

Programs do have bugs (this means that under certain conditions the program will not work properly and damage to the data files may result). All commercial programs are exhaustively tested before being sold, however no testing procedure will cover every possible situation.

To avoid most of these problems buy software that has been available for some time (so someone else will have found the bugs). Again regular backups will limit the damage caused.

Operator errors

It is inevitable that mistakes will be made by the people using the computer system. For example they may input incorrect data.

To minimise this, buy programs that are idiot proofed (as far as possible) and train the staff properly, even if this initially costs money and time it is considerably less expensive than coping with the results of a lack of training.

Only authorised individuals should be able to alter the data in files, others should only be able to read the information but not change it.

Other types of operator error include the failure to carry out backup procedures regularly and effectively, or to do something silly like turning off the computer in the middle of entering the week's invoices.

Another common mistake is to empty coffee over the processor or discs (which may in fact be malicious). Perhaps employees should be encouraged to drink coffee elsewhere, remember that they will work more efficiently if they have regular breaks from the system.

Training is the real answer to minimizing operator errors and you should also check that backup procedures are being carried out correctly and regularly. Ideally one individual should be in control of all security procedures (preferably someone with your complete trust and confidence).

Burglary and theft
Having good insurance and keeping backups off site are ways of limiting the damage to the business from burglars and thieves.

You should carry insurance against these problems as well as the normal contents insurance. You may be able to get insurance that covers the consequential loss arising from the incident.

Backing up files
You will have noticed the consistent mention of taking backups. This was deliberate as the most effective security is to regularly backup your data files onto floppy disc.

This should work on the basis of keeping at least three generations of backups. Each set of backup files should be kept in a separate location (at least one being kept away from the office).

The generations work like this:

*   A backup is made using a new set of discs.

*   Next day (week) another set of backups is made

*   The following day (week) a third set is made

*   The fourth day (week) the first set is re-used

*   The fifth day (week) the second set is re-used and so on.

So whether you choose to back up daily or weekly (or in between) you are keeping three sets of backups on the go.

How often you choose to backup and how many sets of backup discs are kept depends upon your level of paranoia and how often you alter or add to your data files.

Most backup programs allow a selective backup (for example only to backup those files that have been altered since the last backup) this uses less floppy discs to store the backup on and is less time consuming.

> **Every so often it is worth carrying out a full backup of the hard disc.**

There are several backup programs available, some of which are easier to use than the backup program that comes with DOS.

If it takes too long to backup onto floppy disc then it is possible to buy alternative backup media. Tape streamers are available which backup files quickly but have a reputation for being slightly unreliable and optical storage media is becoming more cost effective.

Another option is to backup onto another hard disc (although this means the backups are still physically with the system and consequently more vulnerable).

Network security

There are certain security procedures which only apply to network systems. In a network the individual workstations communicate with each other and share resources (e.g. printers, hard discs), the possibilities of problems occurring are greater.

If you have a network system then please pay particular attention to the effective use of passwords. Also consider the following:

* Which users should be able to look at which files and who should be able to change the contents of files.

* Is it necessary to lock the network server away to prevent the wrong individuals accessing the network from the server (by booting it directly into DOS).

* Think about buying workstations without floppy disc drives. This will prevent illegal copying of files and will prevent employees introducing games and possibly viruses into the system.

* Only allow the named network manager to have access to the server. Inexperienced users have been known to format hard discs on stand alone systems, think how much more damage formatting a network hard disc could do.

* It might be worthwhile purchasing an UPS (uninterruptable power supply) for the network server. This means that if the power fails the server is closed down safely, with files being closed and all necessary data saved to disc.

* It is also a good idea to buy special programs that will test the network system and identify problems before they can cause damage.

Virus detection and prevention

Although viruses are a topic of conversation and concern among computer users, it is still true to say that the actual incidence of viral attacks on computer systems is small (although growing). This is no consolation to someone experiencing a virus attack of course, so I would suggest being very careful.

I recently found a system infected with the Tequila virus which while relatively benign and which did not trash the files completely, did involve considerable thought and effort in eradicating it. It could have been far worse, so be vigilant.

How to infect your system with a virus
Copy an infected file onto your hard disc and then run it.

Using any infected floppy disc (be very careful about demo discs and any disc that has not come from a totally reputable source).

By downloading or copying programs from dubious sources such as bulletin boards.

How to minimize your chances of being infected
Do not do any of the above.

All incoming discs should be checked by the person having overall responsibility for security by using special anti-viral programs to scan them for viruses. These scanning programs can also be used to examine an existing system for known viruses and will report any damage caused. This includes scanning commercial programs as well as demonstration programs, games and shareware.

Install some form of password protection so that the system cannot be used by anyone not knowing the password. Some computer systems have these as standard and so do some operating systems (e.g. DRDOS6).

Anti-viral techniques

Scanning programs will only check for known viruses, and need frequent updates to keep up to date with the new viruses being written. Virus authors tend to write new viruses once the original is capable of being checked by the virus scanning program.

Another method of locating viruses is the checksum program. This works by looking at the files and calculating a checksum based on the data in the file. When the program is run again, it recalculates the checksum figure to see that it is the same and can thus identify those files that have been altered by a virus as the value of the checksum will have changed.

A further approach is the sentry type program. This checks any attempt to write to the hard disc. If an attempt is made to alter a program file, then it is stopped (you are given the opportunity to let the write to disc carry on). This is very satisfactory for program files but not for data files.

Once a virus has infected a system, then it will need to be removed. Anti-viral programs will identify the infected files and try to remove the infection without damaging the file. Again the anti-viral program must be kept up to date.

Sometimes it is necessary to reformat the hard disc and reinstall the files (from uninfected copies).

It is probably true that for every clever anti-viral program, some person will write a virus program that will outwit it. By definition anti-viral programs are one step behind.

Signs that your system has been attacked by a virus

Here are some indications of a viral attack:

* Programs begin to take much longer than normal to load and / or so does accessing data files (try defragmenting your disc files first though).

* Programs that used to run successfully crash or won't load.

* System memory shrinks.

* Unknown messages begin to appear (although DOS has some pretty strange ones of its own).

* Files begin to disappear and then re-appear.

* Strange and wondrous phenomena occur (when using programs with which you are very familiar).

However unusual happenings are still statistically far more likely to be the result of hardware or software problems rather than viral infections.

Some of the leading anti-viral programs are Alan Solomon's Toolkit, Norton Anti-Virus and Centre Point Anti-Virus.

If you do become infected, there are several firms who will clear your system and try to repair your infected files (some work on a no success, no fee basis). One of the best known authorities in this field is Alan Solomons who is often found writing articles on the subject.

Final advice

Whatever you do, don't panic, always think the problem through before attempting to do anything. Ideally get to some point in the program you are using and exit, then close down the system and have a think. You may wish to call in the experts.

If you buy **and use regularly** two anti-virus programs then you are likely to avoid any problems. It is better to use two since tests show that no single program will discover all viruses. However nothing is 100% safe.

Notes:

All program files should be copied before use and the masters kept safely (this is normal operating procedure and all program documentation tells you to do this).

Always backup your files regularly and keep several generations of backup discs.

The auditing of accounts

It is necessary for all financial records, whether computerised or not, to have an audit trail. This simply means being able to trace a transaction from start to finish, for example from when an item was originally purchased to when it was sold. Any business that needs to have its accounts audited must ensure that an adequate audit trail is kept.

It is always best to discuss this with your accountant before buying and installing programs that will be used to keep your firm's financial records. He or she may have views on which accounting programs would be most suitable for your business (if your accountant uses or is familiar with a specific program which he recommends then this is likely to be the best one to get since he will be able to help you use it and there may be a consequent reduction in your accountancy fees).

This presumes you have faith in your accountant and that he or she is computer literate.

It is also worth checking with the Institute of Chartered Accountants and the Inland Revenue for their opinion of the proposed program (is it one they recognise).

The Law

When buying a system

There is some protection given to you by consumer law. Broadly the product has to conform to the following:

Be of merchantable quality
It must work and it must be complete as described by the supplier and in the advertising. Obviously if this description is not written down then there can be a problem.

Fit for the purpose for which it was supplied
If you (preferably in writing) say you want the system to do a particular activity, then it must be able to do it. You are relying on the expertise of the seller to provide you with the correct product.

Obviously if it doesn't work, is not exactly what you ordered or is broken, then you can return it for a full refund (it should be returned within seven days of purchase). You do not have to have it fixed if you do not want to, however if you do agree to have it mended then you cannot later ask for your money back.

Try to pay by credit card as you have some protection from the credit card company if the supplier goes out of business or there are other problems.

If buying by mail order always put the order in writing and keep a copy.

If at all goes horribly wrong
Well at least you have everything in writing so when you institute legal proceedings you have proof.

Organizations to approach are firstly the credit card company, then any of the following, the citizens advice centre, a solicitor or the small claims court.

You might also like to contact the magazine you saw the advertisement in (this applies particularly if you bought by mail order).

Most problems can be easily sorted out between you and your supplier if approached in the right spirit.

The Data Protection Act and you

This legislation is designed to protect the individual against the misuse of personal data. Unfortunately it also affects any organization or business keeping facts about people on computer file.

The eight principles of the Act are:

*   Data should be obtained fairly and lawfully.

*   The data should be held for specified purposes.

*   The data should not be used for other purposes.

*   The data should be adequate, relevant, and only as much data should be kept as is necessary for the stated purposes.

*   The data must be accurate and up to date.

*   The data should only be kept as long as necessary.

*   Individuals are entitled to see their data and where appropriate to have it corrected or amended.

*   Appropriate security procedures must be taken to guard against unauthorised access to, modification of, disclosure of or destruction of the data.

Manual records are excluded from the act, so if you keep your customer database on a card index, the DPA does not apply. If you keep the data on a computer then you have to register. There are certain exemptions, but anyone else holding personal details on a computer has to register under the Act.

Personal data is data from which a living human being can be identified. Limited companies and the dead are not covered by the Act.

If you intend to pass the data onto a third party this must be stated when you register.

It costs £75 (1992) to register for three years and forms to register can be obtained from the Data Protection Registrars office at Wilmslow.

Booklets detailing the Act are available by phone (0625 535777), these are free.

Exemptions

Individuals not running a business and clubs can keep computer records without registering, provided certain conditions are fulfilled, and businesses can keep the payroll on computer without registering provided the information is not used for any other purposes.

If you have a list of names and addresses from which you send out a mail-shot or other information then you do not have to register provided no-one on the list objects. If you put additional details besides the name and address then you have to register.

After reading the detailed booklets and the registration form, if you are still unsure whether you need to register or not then a letter to the registrar outlining the data you intend to keep and the purposes you intend to use it for will clarify the position for you.

There are financial penalties for those who do not register when they should have done so.

Sources of Information

You can find more detailed information, prices, etc., from a variety of sources, here are some of them.

Magazines

If you look at a newsagents magazine rack, the number and variety of computer magazines is startling. A new title seems to appear almost every month.

Magazines tend to be directed at a specific target audience and can be split into several main groups, those aimed at owners (or prospective owners) of odd makes of computer (e.g. Amstrad PCW - an excellent word processing machine but with limited potential for anything else), games players and business users.

You are interested in magazines aimed primarily at business and here are some examples of this type of magazine to give a flavour of what is available.

COMPUTER BUYER
As its name suggests aimed at the prospective buyer with the usual mix of reviews and articles.

COMPUTER SHOPPER
Amazing value if you want the advertisements. Also contains useful and interesting technical articles. A great (in every sense) read.

PC ANSWERS
Contains very informative articles on both hardware and software, explaining them sensibly and lucidly. Also answers readers' questions on a variety of topics.

PC PLUS

From the same publisher as PC ANSWERS, this magazine gives away a free disc full of programs every month (in fact this is an increasing ploy by publishers desperate to sell copies in a highly competitive market, you may decide which magazine to buy each month from the contents of the free disc).

PERSONAL COMPUTER WORLD

Aimed primarily at the business world and again containing a useful mix of technical articles and reviews of new products.

PC DIRECT

This is aimed at the direct buyer (i.e. one who buys by mail order to obtain the lowest price). It contains many advertisements and offers advice to its readership. It also contains useful articles on various aspects of computing.

The best way for you to choose a magazine is to go to the newsagents and look through all those available. Choose the ones which you find easy to read and pitched at the level you need.

Sources of training

These can be very variable, both in price and quality of the product. The most cost effective and accessible will be either the local college (phone for advice on the courses available) or your dealer (who may well include some training with the overall system). Remember that both can offer courses specifically tailored to your needs as well as the courses they advertise.

There are also specialist training firms operating in the bigger towns and cities who advertise in the trade and local press, some of whom offer excellent training.

Whenever you buy training it is very advisable to be as clear as possible (preferably in writing) about the details of exactly what is being provided (contents, length of course, etc.).

Consultants

You may see advertised in the local press or telephone directory, firms or individuals advertising themselves as computer consultants or advisers.   Again these can be anyone from the extremely knowledgeable and helpful to cowboys.

Before hiring them ask the following:

*   What professional qualifications do they have.

*   What is the length and type of their experience.

*   The names of several recent clients you can phone for a reference.

*   Are they completely independent of suppliers (this is not necessarily a problem if they declare their interests).

*   Their fee structure (how much do they charge).

User groups

These are groups devoted to a type or make of hardware or software. They are supposed to be independent of the manufacturer and can act as a pressure group and as a channel for users' comments to the manufacturer (to the benefit of both the manufacturer and the user). You can find out about them from magazines (perhaps by phoning the editorial offices) and from the manufacturers.

Some user groups work very closely with the manufacturer, while others maintain a distance (in theory to keep their independence). User groups can be a remarkably good source of unbiased advice and assistance with problems.

User groups also provide various services depending on their size and finances, besides giving advice they may publish a newsletter, maintain a bulletin board and run helplines and training courses.

Appendix 1

Extended and expanded RAM memory

As programs became larger there became a need for more RAM. To meet this need, first expanded and then extended memory came into being. It is now possible to distinguish several types of RAM.

Conventional (or base memory)
The first 640K of RAM. It is here that the operating system and the device drivers (e.g. mouse driver) are normally loaded.

The remainder of the 640K is used to load the application program and the data. Under DOS, applications can only run in the first 640K, this is called the 640K barrier.

Upper memory
Any memory addressed between 640K and 1 megabyte is called upper memory. This is 384K in size and is normally used for the video display adapter and the ROM BIOS (sometimes called Shadow RAM).

Some operating systems (DR-DOS5 and 6 and MSDOS5) allow vacant upper memory to be used for installable drivers such as the mouse driver, network card driver or (some) TSR (terminate-stay-resident programs, e.g. Sidekick).

This frees up conventional memory for the application programs. It is also possible with the right operating system or utility to locate the main operating system kernel into upper memory, again freeing conventional memory.

Extended memory
XT's (8088/8086 based processors) are limited to a maximum of 1Mb
RAM. However 80286, 80386 and 80486 based processors are able
to address memory in excess of this.

For these processors to access memory above 1Mb, the processor has
to be in protected mode (when in real mode, 286, 386 and 486
processors are simply running as fast 8086 based machines).

Popular uses for extended memory include RAMdiscs and disc
caches. Again an operating system capable of accessing extended
memory is needed.

Some programs (e.g. Windows 3) can access extended memory
directly and are not restricted to the 640K barrier.

Memory management programs (e.g. Qemm or 386Max) allow
memory above 1Mb to be configured as extended or expanded
memory.

High memory area (HMA)
High memory is the first 64K of extended memory. This is only
available on 286, 386 and 486 machines and can be used to load the
main operating system kernel.

XMS
XMS (Extended memory specification) was developed by Lotus, Intel
and Microsoft to provide a standard interface to upper, high and
extended memory. Up to 15Mbytes of extended memory can be
addressed on 286 machines and up to 1000Mbytes on 386 and 486
machines.

Expanded memory

An alternative to extended memory is to use expanded memory . The LIM EMS was devised by Lotus, Intel and Microsoft (EMS means expanded memory specification). Expanded memory was originally developed to overcome the memory limitations of XT (8086) machines. The latest version is LIM 4.0.

Expanded memory allows large programs to run which would not run as efficiently in conventional memory.

Up to 32Mbytes of memory outside of conventional memory can be addressed, and it is particularly useful for programs that need to access large amounts of data, e.g. spreadsheets and database programs.

However due to its method of accessing the memory above 1Mb, expanded memory is slower than extended memory, and is really only useful with programs that cannot work with extended memory.

Appendix 2

VGA resolutions

These figures are maximum figures, the monitor may not be capable of these resolutions even if the graphics adaptor card is.

RAM on the card	Resolution	No of colours
256K	640 x 480 pixels	256
	800 x 600	16
512K	800 x 600	256
	1024 x 768	16
1024K	1024 x 768	256

Appendix 3

Common computing terms

Alphanumeric
A character, either a numeral, a letter or other symbol.

Application (program)
A program which is used for a (business) task.

Architecture
How the various parts of the hardware are arranged together.

Artificial intelligence
An attempt to produce a computer system that can learn by its own experience and therefore has intelligence. It does depend how intelligence is defined of course.

ASCII (American Standard Code for Information Interchange).
The normal way keyboard characters are coded. Most DOS manuals contain an ASCII code set as an appendix.

AT
This stands for advanced technology and is the term used by IBM (and clone manufacturers) to describe the technological advance from XT machines.

Backup
Copying files from a hard disc onto floppy disc (or a tape streamer). This is done in case something dreadful happens to the original (and it will).

BASIC

Standing for Beginners All Purpose Symbolic Instructions Code, this is one of the easiest computer languages to learn (if only because you can write your first program within half an hour or so of starting). In its more structured forms it is used as a professional programming language.

Baud rate

A measurement of the speed that data is transmitted over telephone lines.

Benchmark

A series of tests carried out on systems to calculate their performance. They are useful for comparing one machine to another but only if the same version of the benchmark test is used.

BIOS

The Basic Input/Output System. This is stored in ROM and controls activities like screen displays.

Bit / Byte

Characters are stored as binary digits (bits) in the computer. A byte is eight bits and represents one of our characters. Thus if the storage of a disc is expressed in so many millions of bytes (megabytes) it gives an indication of how many characters can be stored. For reference a Kb or kilobyte is 1024 bytes.

Boot up

This is the start up procedure when a computer is switched on and the initial software is loaded from ROM.

Buffer

A temporary memory area. For example a printer buffer will hold data from the CPU so that the CPU can continue with its work and not be held up waiting for the printer to finish.

Bug

An error (normally in a program) which causes unusual results or even system crashes. To remove errors is called debugging.

Bus
Data and program instructions are transferred along the bus on their way to and from the processor.

CAD
Computer Aided Design, used for industrial purposes and also by architects.

CD-Rom
A new storage medium. Used to store massive amounts of data which can then be read by the computer. Information on CD-ROM cannot be altered (at present).

Chip
Made of silicon on which are the electronic circuits.

Clock
There is an internal clock in the computer which synchronises the activities of the system.

Clone
A word used to describe any IBM compatible computer, i.e. one which will run the same software as a genuine IBM.

Comms
Short for communications.

CPU
The Central Processing Unit. This is the heart of the system and interprets program instructions and issues commands to the rest of the system to ensure the program is carried out.

Cursor
A symbol (normally a line) indicating where typing will appear on the screen.

Documentation
Normally supplied with both hardware and programs. It has been known to be less than adequate especially for a beginner. Be warned.

Email
Short for electronic mail.

Expansion slot
A socket inside the system box into which an expansion card can be plugged (e.g. for an internal modem).

Expert system
A program which stores certain rules drawn up by human experts in their particular subject (e.g. a doctor). The idea is that the expert system can then answer routine questions as well as (possibly better than) the human expert. This has been tried with some success in medicine among other areas.

Firmware
Used to describe programs stored on a ROM chip.

Font
A particular design and size of character. Most printers can print several different fonts in different sizes. A scaleable font means a character design available in any size rather than certain fixed sizes.

Graphics
Pictures, charts, really anything other than letters or numbers. The term graphics mode means that the screen will display underlining, etc., properly.

GUI
Graphical User Interface which uses icons (pictures) in place of text, e.g. Windows 3.

Hardcopy
Printed output

Hardware
The physical bits and pieces of the system.

High level language
These are programming languages which are supposed to be as near as possible to our normal language. To be used they have to be compiled (translated) into machine code (which is the language the computer actually understands).

Interleave factor

This can affect how fast programs and data can be accessed from the hard disc. This is normally preset. Certain utilities (e.g. Norton) can optimize the interleave factor. Please note that IDE drives are preset and you should **NOT** try to change the interleave factor (most systems now use IDE hard discs).

Joystick

A device used to control games. Most games can use a mouse or keyboard though.

Macro

A series of keystrokes recorded as a file which can be replayed at will. This allows an element of automation to repetitive tasks.

Menu

A series of choices often in the form of a pull-down menu.

Modem

A MOdulator/DEModulator, used to translate the computer's language into a form that can be transmitted along phone lines and then translated back at the other end.

Monitor

Another name for a VDU (visual display unit).

Mouse

A device which is moved around the desk; the pointer on the screen moves in relation to the movement of the mouse on the desk.

Multi-media

The use of computer technology together with film and sound to produce an overall presentation.

Multi-tasking

Carrying on more than one task at the same time. Only available on PC's with a 80386 processor and the necessary software.

Numeric keypad

Normally on the far right of the keyboard, it is very useful for entering figures (and much faster).

Peripheral
Any hardware device other than the CPU (central processing unit).

Pixel
The screen is made up of thousands of pixels or dots and characters are formed from these dots (which is why on some lowish quality screens it is possible to easily see the dots making up each character).

PostScript
A page description language used with laser printers and by typesetters.

Ports
These can be either serial or parallel and are sockets at the back of the computer into which are connected peripherals such as printers or mice, etc.

Program
A series of precise instructions telling the system how to carry out a task.

Prompt
A symbol on the screen marking the position to type a response or issue a command, e.g. the DOS prompt.

PSU
Power supply unit.

QWERTY
The normal layout of the keyboard.

RAM
Random Access Memory. Used to store program instructions and the data used by the program while the program is being run (carried out). RAM loses its contents when the power is switched off.

Resolution
This means the number of dots making up the rows and columns displayed on the screen. Thus 800 x 600 means 800 dots (across) by 600 dots (up).

ROM

Read Only Memory, this is memory that cannot be altered and is used for the BIOS among other things.

SIPPS and SIMS

RAM memory on miniature circuit boards. They are connected to sockets on the computer's main board (motherboard), and are used to add to the RAM capacity of the processor.

String

A character string, i.e. any set of characters that is not a number.

Syntax error

A mistake in the use of a language or operating system. Normally a grammatical error in the construction of a command or program statement.

Toner

Laser printers use toner to print (it is a black powder).

TSR

Terminate and Stay Resident programs. They remain in RAM even when not being used and so are quickly available when needed. Normally these are small but useful programs (for example an on-screen calculator or appointments diary or a virus checker).

Video card

A card containing the circuits to run the monitor in whatever mode is required (e.g. VGA).

WIMP

This stands for Windows, Icons, Mice and Pull down Menus. They form part of the new GUI's like Windows 3.

XT

The original PC standard, rather old technology now, though perfectly usable for tasks such as word processing.

Index

A
accounting, 6,7,8,25,26,27,28,29,41,46,48,92
application, 13,14,15,19,34,35,38,39,40,49,50,57,59,70,73,100,104
architecture, 73,104
audit, 28,92

B
backup, 18,44,73,82,84,85,86,91,104
buffers, 61,105
buying, 1,4,6,8,18,21,26,45,50,73,87,92,93

C
cache, 15,51,54,101
CAD, 49,106
CD Rom, 62
charting, 30,31
comms, 36,75,106
consultant, 3,4,5,99
contract, 5,6,7,8,11,12,84

D
Data Protection Act (DPA), 69,95,96
database, 30,32,33,34,35,36,46,48,70,75,80,95,102
disk controller, 57
documentation, 9,11,91,106
DOS, 13,14,15,16,17,22,38,40,46,49,50,52,86,87,88,100,109
dtp, 23,57

E
EEC, 64,69
expansion, 54,57,58,62,71,76,107

N
network, 28,49,65,70,71,72,73,74,75,87,100
noise, 60,66,67,71

O
operating system, 13,14,16,18,38,41,46,71,74,88,100,101,110

P
passwords, 15,71,72,78,79,83,87,88
pixel, 56,103,109
print driver, 20
printers,
7,20,23,24,42,48,60,61,65,66,68,70,71,74,82,87,105,107,109,110
processor,
14,24,35,39,40,48,49,50,51,54,56,61,62,71 84,101,106,108,110

R
radiation, 64,68,69
RAM, 24,39,40,42,48,49,50,54,100,101,103,109,110
reports, 21,24,25,28,30,32,34,44
resolution, 55,56,57,103
ROM, 50,62,100,105,106,107,110

S
scanner, 42,62
security, 28,29,33,72,73,81,85,87,88,95
shareware, 42,43,45,46,47,77,88
software,
2,4,6,7,11,13,41,45,47,49,52,54,62,71,72,73,75,84,97,99,105,106,108
spreadsheet, 20,29,30,31,34,36,40,42,46,57,60,102

T
training, 2,5,7,10,24,84,85,98,99
TSR, 100,110

V
VDU, 6,16,64
VGA, 55,56,57,58,103,110
video display, 55,100
virus, 46,73,77,87,88,89,90,91,110